The Elements
AETHER

JUSTYN TIME

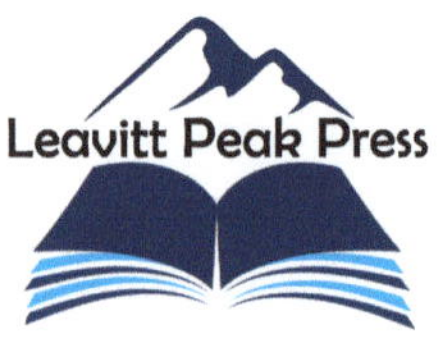

ISBN: 978-1-962363-33-4 (sc)
ISBN: 978-1-962363-34-1 (e)

Rev. date: 12/07/2023

Introduction

Greek mythology believed that the Aether was the God of light. It was also believed that the light could be manipulated through the use of gravity. The gravity could be directed with that of a virtual tube or writing instrument to create words, letters or drawings. It is the author's opinion that he now has proof or evidence of the existence of the Aether.

The images contained within this visual publication are a representation of the evidence. You are invited to delve deep into the multi-layered imagery inside the pages of the elements-Aether. The God of the heavens is magical and beyond comprehension. There is nothing that He cannot accomplish. His abilities are beyond what we could ever imagine or dream of. The infinite beauty, creativity and thoughts of our Adonai will never be contained or restrained within the dome of our cranium. He is the Alpha and Omega, the Beginning and the End. He is not limited by time, space or matter. Father, Son and Holy Spirit.

Believer or not, the imagery presented here will challenge the viewer to look at our physical world with spiritual vision. May your eyes be opened into the realm of the impossible, because that is where our God resides. There are dragons, magi, wise men and women hidden within these images. Our Father in heaven is full of loving grace, mercy, forgiveness and redemption. His redeeming power transformed the life, body, soul and spirit of Justyn Time. This happened right on time to change his world in more than subtle ways. When his world changed, that of his friends and family members' lives changed as well. Is it truly possible for one man to change the course of history? It happened with Jesus and by the direction of Jesus it has happened once again in the life of the author.

We Triple Dog Dare you to stare at each image for 33 seconds, undistracted by electronics or your normal routine. Thus allowing the multi-layered imagery to come to life right before your eyes. Sit back, have a glass of wine, some gummies, enjoy some cannabis or meditate with your favorite music on. Do whatever it is that brings you into close proximity with your God and creator. Then enjoy the visual feast as you explore the Aether as only God can create it.

If you or someone you know suffers from anxiety or depression, these images have been known to be calming, encouraging, awe inspiring and even breathtaking. The following is a description of how and where, San Jose California, the images were created. By God and his angels working within the elements - Aether.

1. Some images are sunlight reflected off of the cars and trucks just prior to sunset. The reflections then land upon the walls and ceiling of the carports.
2. Some are sunlight reflections off of the rims of cars and trucks cast onto the asphalt.
3. Some are of sunlight reflected off of the windows of apartments and then cast onto the wall of a nearby building approximately 100 feet away.
4. Still other images are created by sunlight being filtered through the tree branches and leaves that are then drawn upon a wall or fence.
5. Another way the images have been created has been from sunlight being reflected off of the back of a work truck. The images were then cast upon a concrete wall.
6. The final way this has been created was one of the first and most profound ways. Headlights from a parked car or sometimes two were cast across a span of approximately 150 feet to hit the window. The light was then reflected towards another wall that is approximately another 100 feet away. This light then created a detailed drawing of what appears to be a cocoon in the midst of a storm. The impossible is made possible by the God that I know and have been personally saved by.

This God is the artist of my heart and soul! I am the photographer and pupil of His mastery.

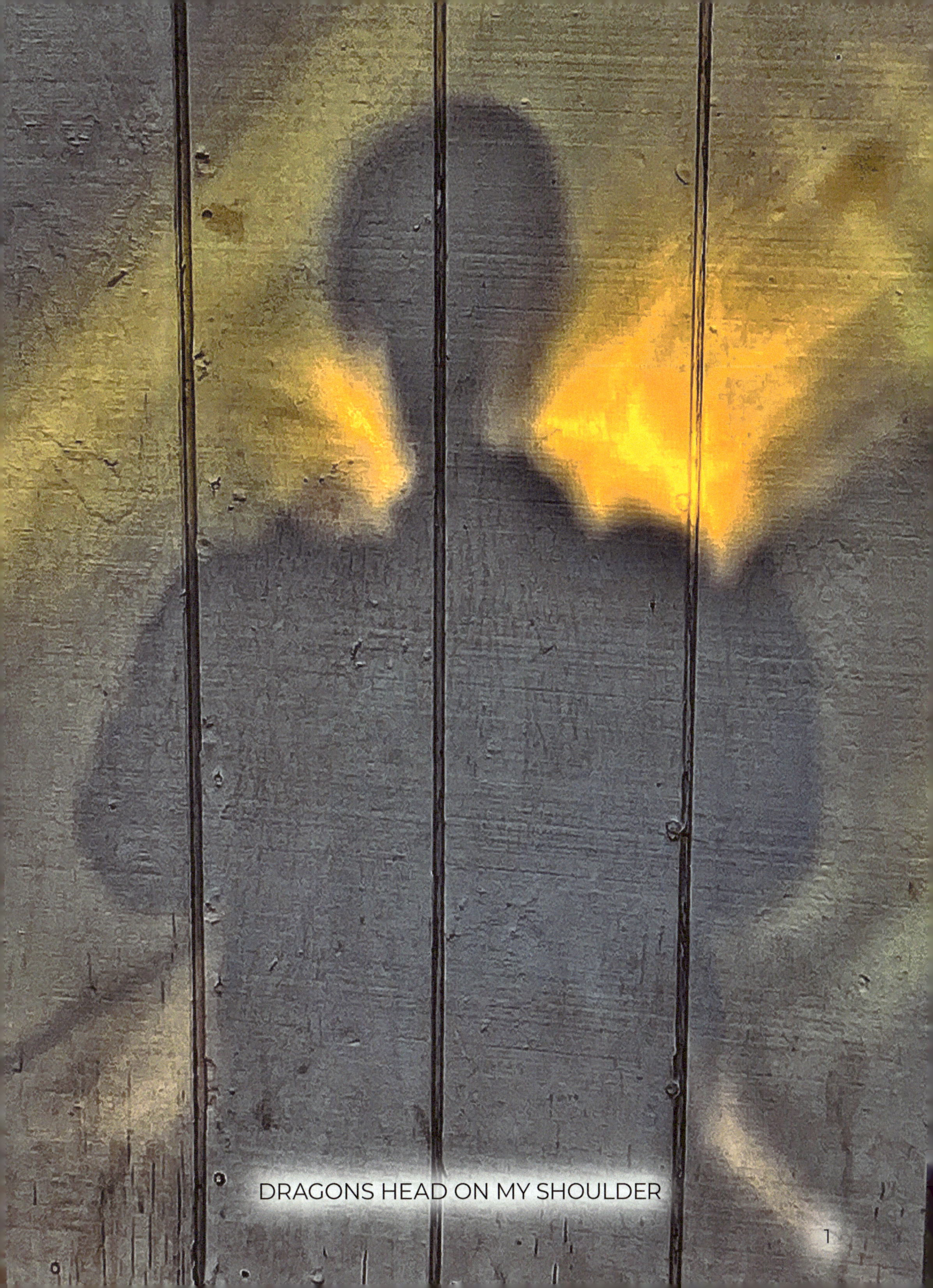
DRAGONS HEAD ON MY SHOULDER

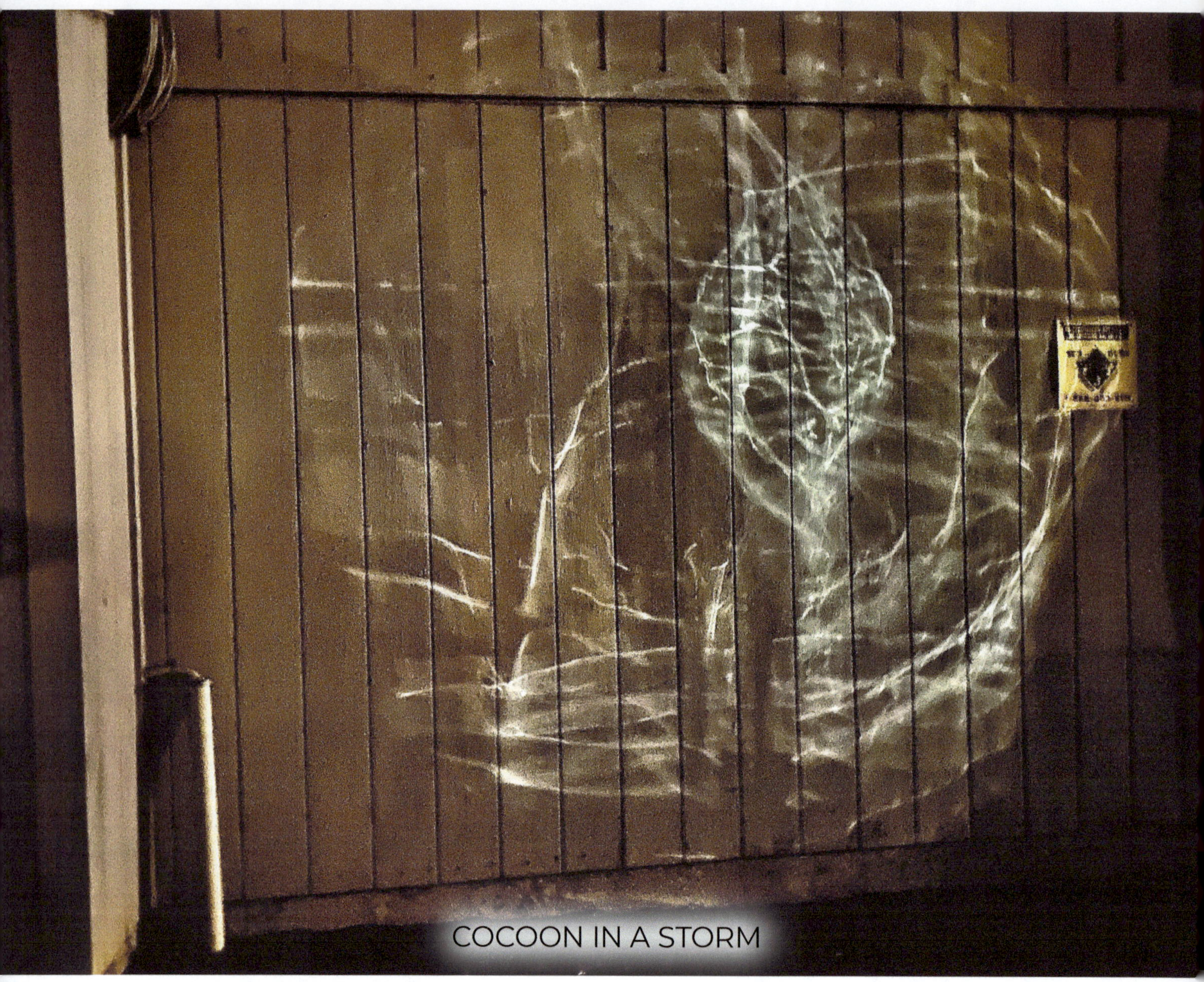

COCOON IN A STORM

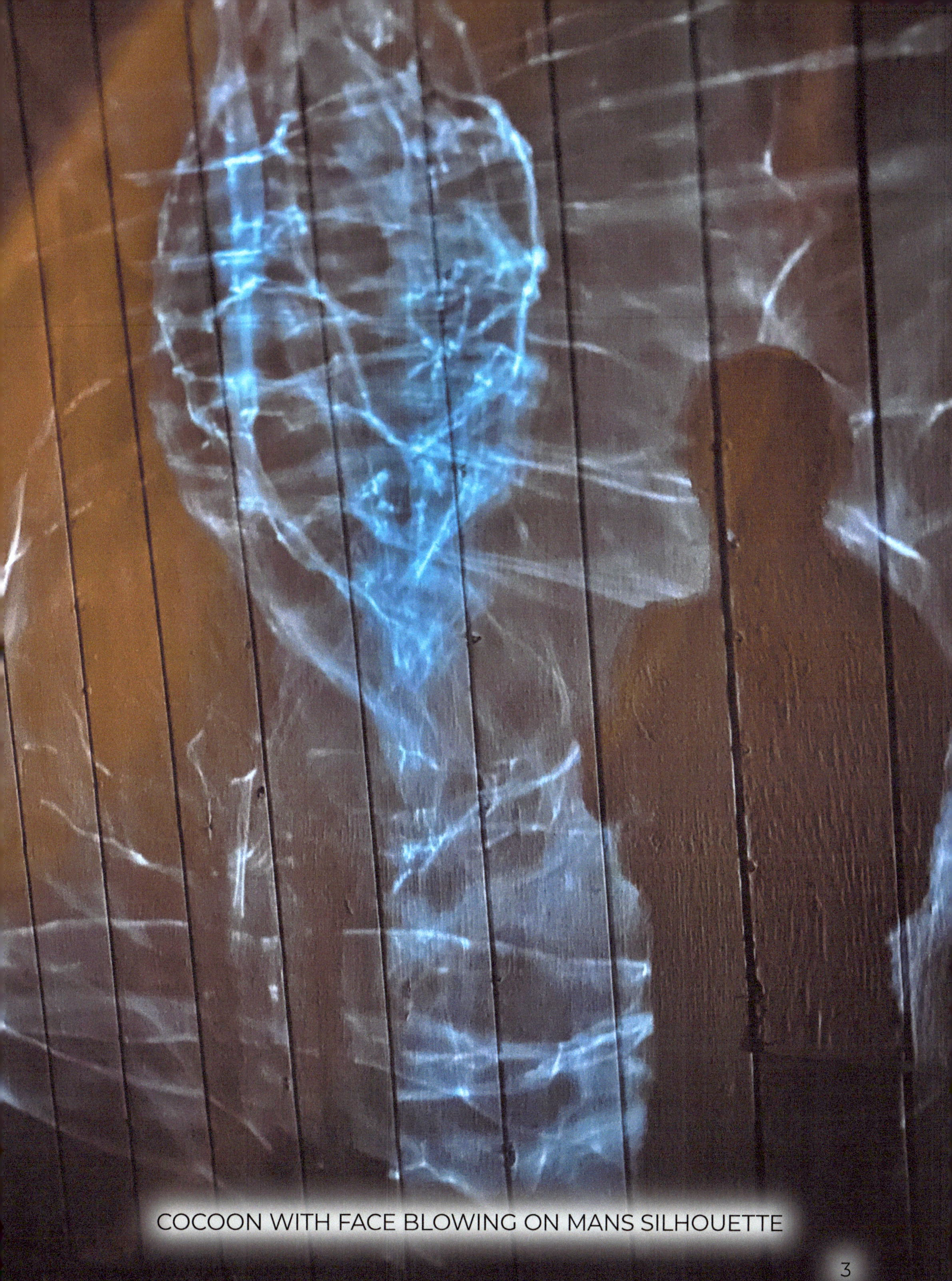

COCOON WITH FACE BLOWING ON MANS SILHOUETTE

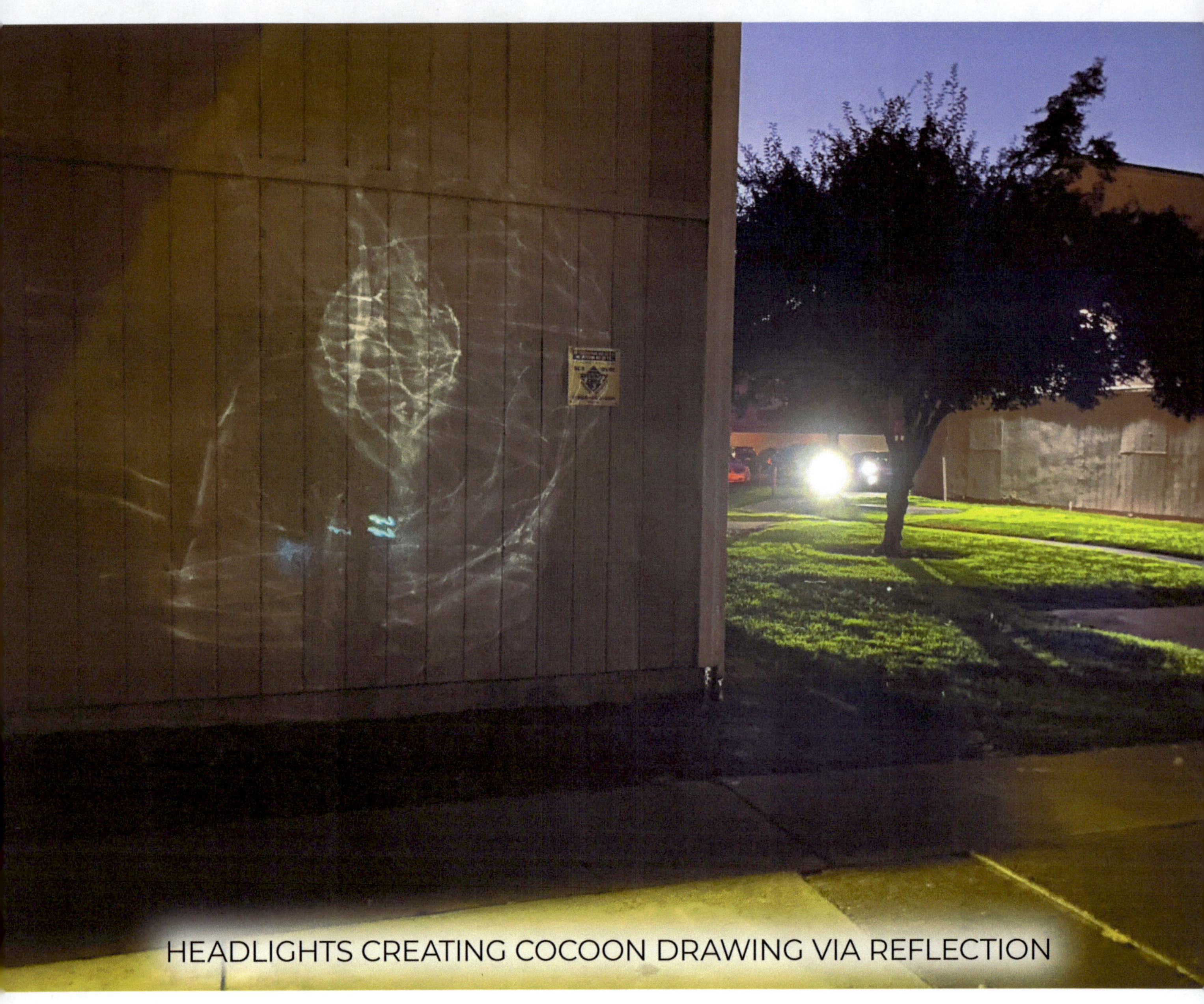

HEADLIGHTS CREATING COCOON DRAWING VIA REFLECTION

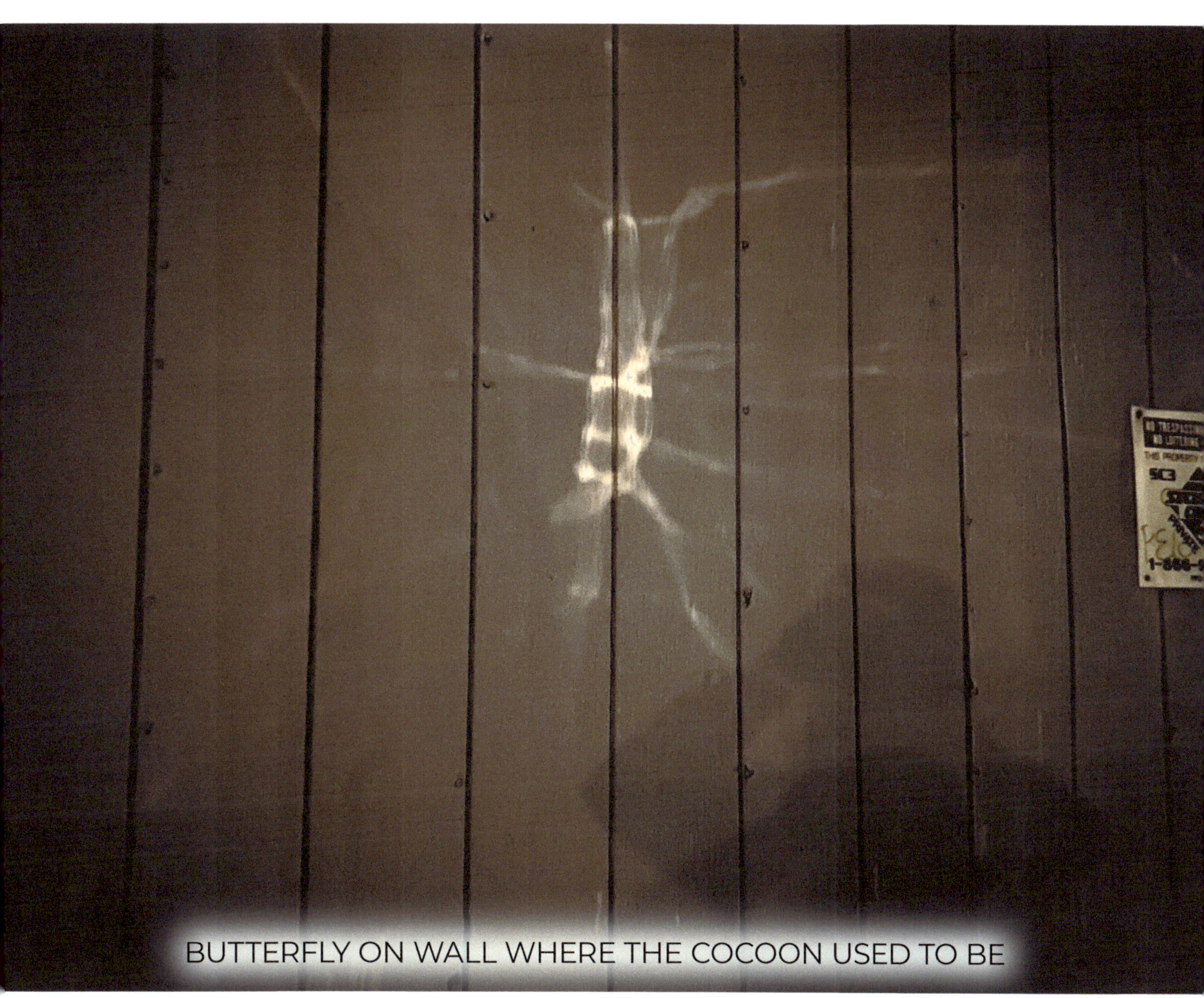

BUTTERFLY ON WALL WHERE THE COCOON USED TO BE

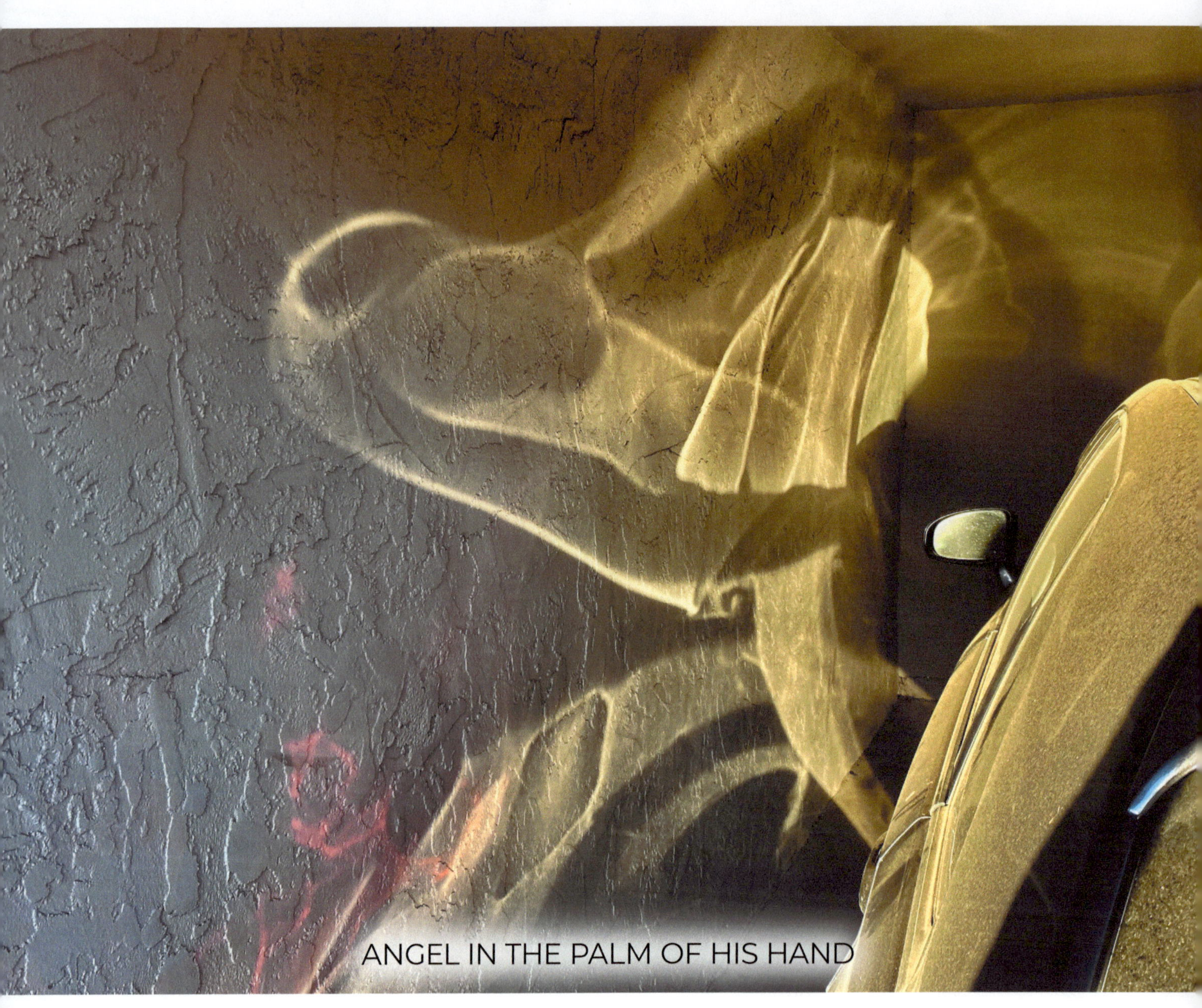
ANGEL IN THE PALM OF HIS HAND

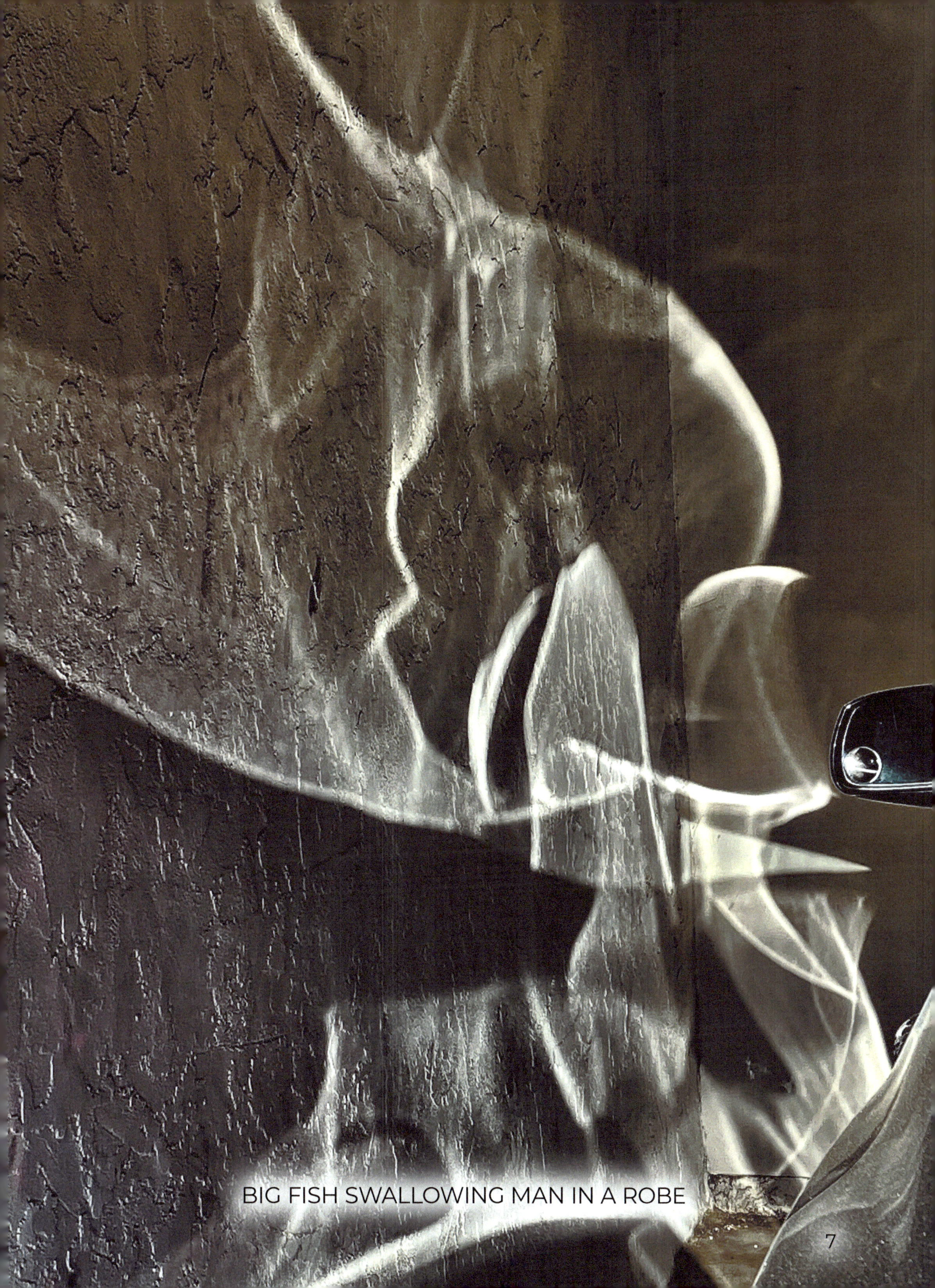

BIG FISH SWALLOWING MAN IN A ROBE

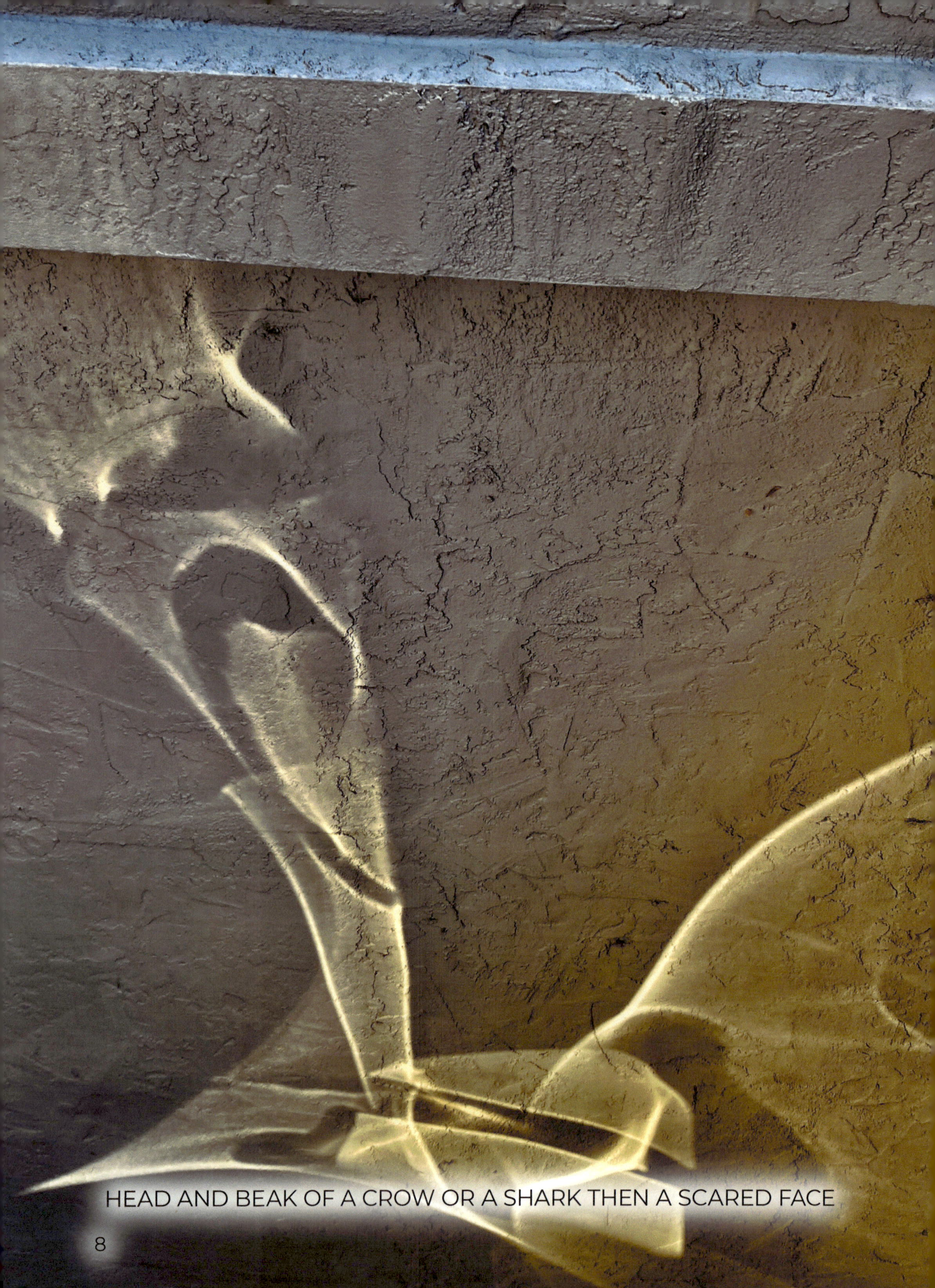

HEAD AND BEAK OF A CROW OR A SHARK THEN A SCARED FACE

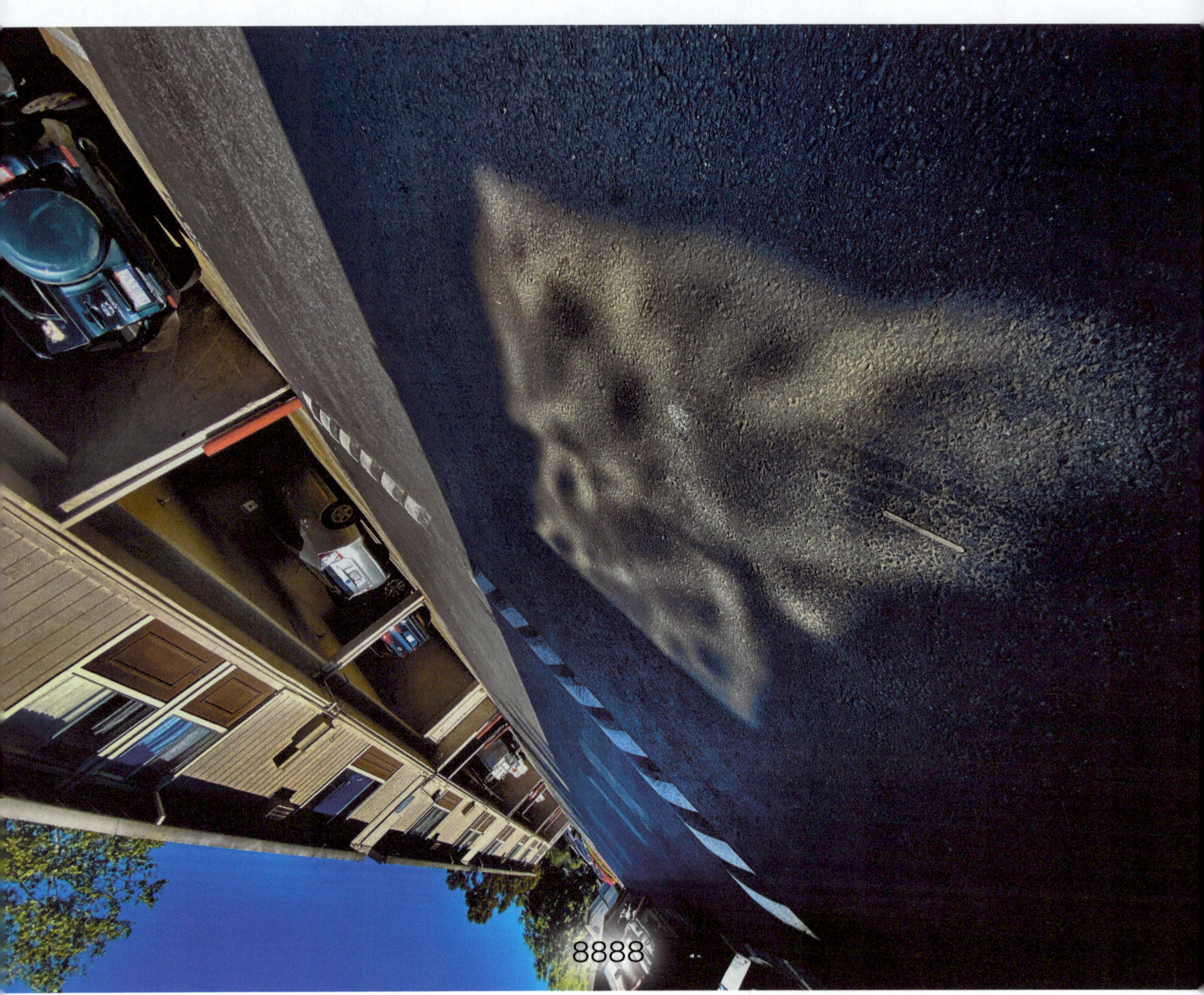

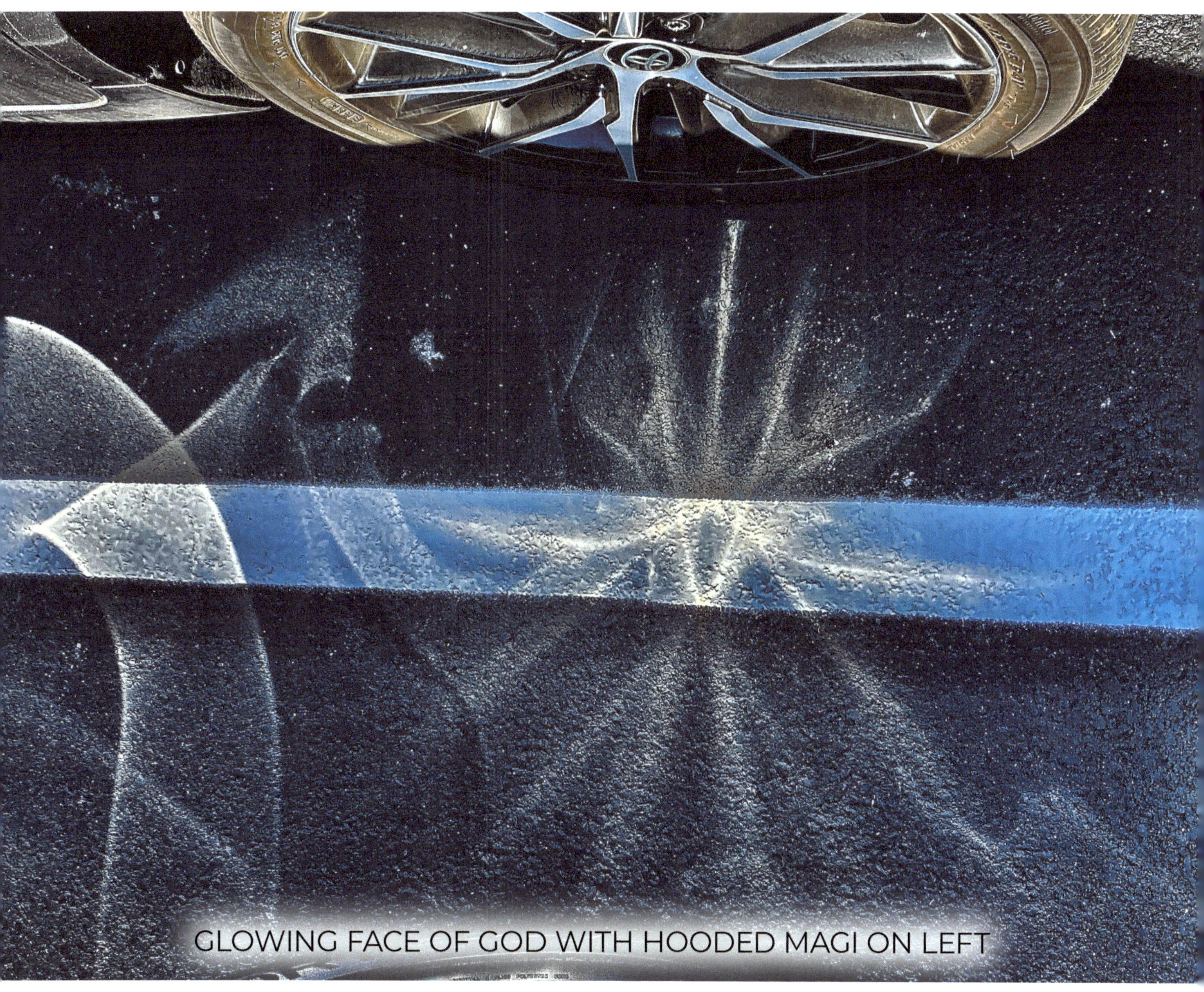

GLOWING FACE OF GOD WITH HOODED MAGI ON LEFT

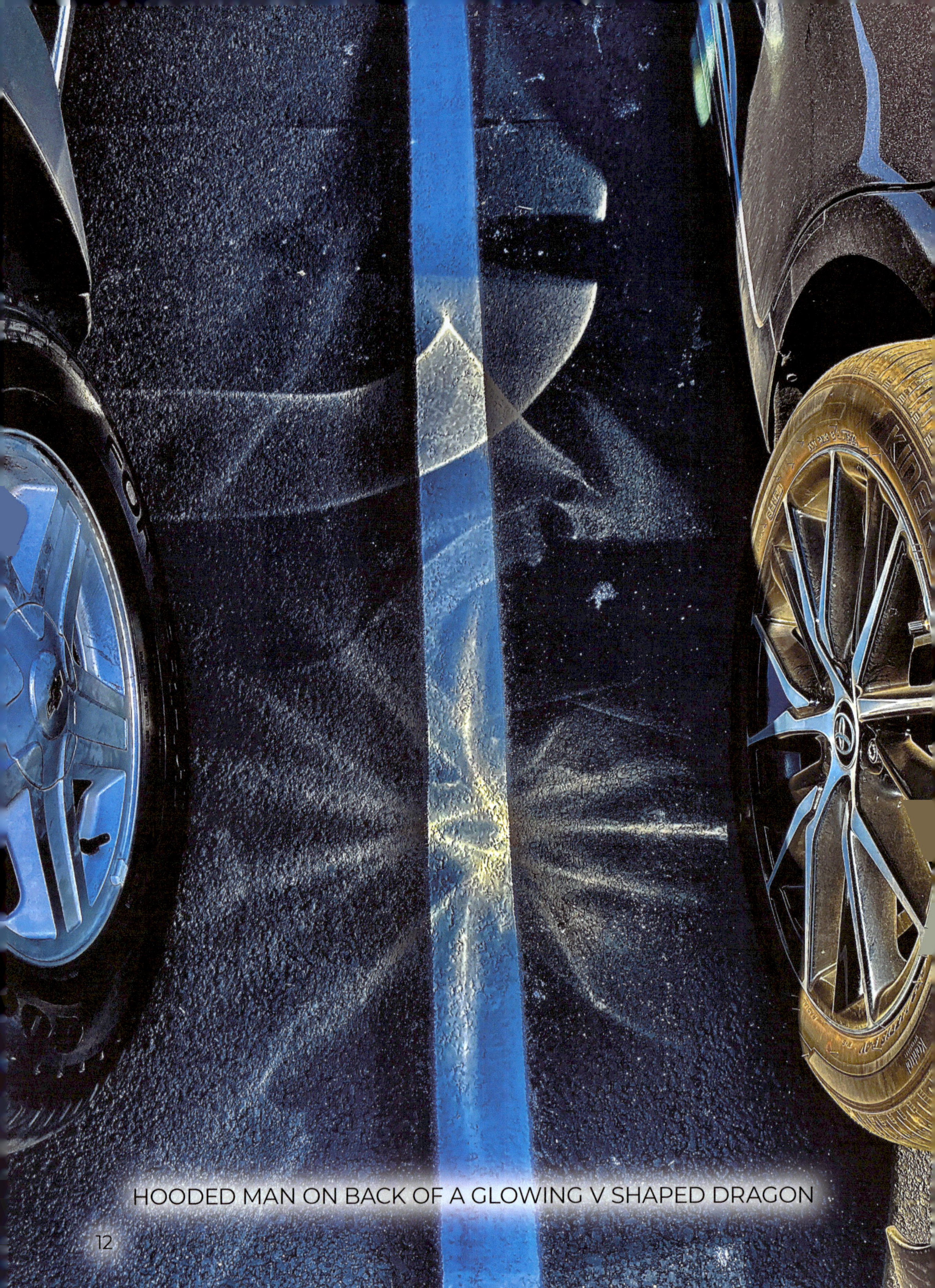

HOODED MAN ON BACK OF A GLOWING V SHAPED DRAGON

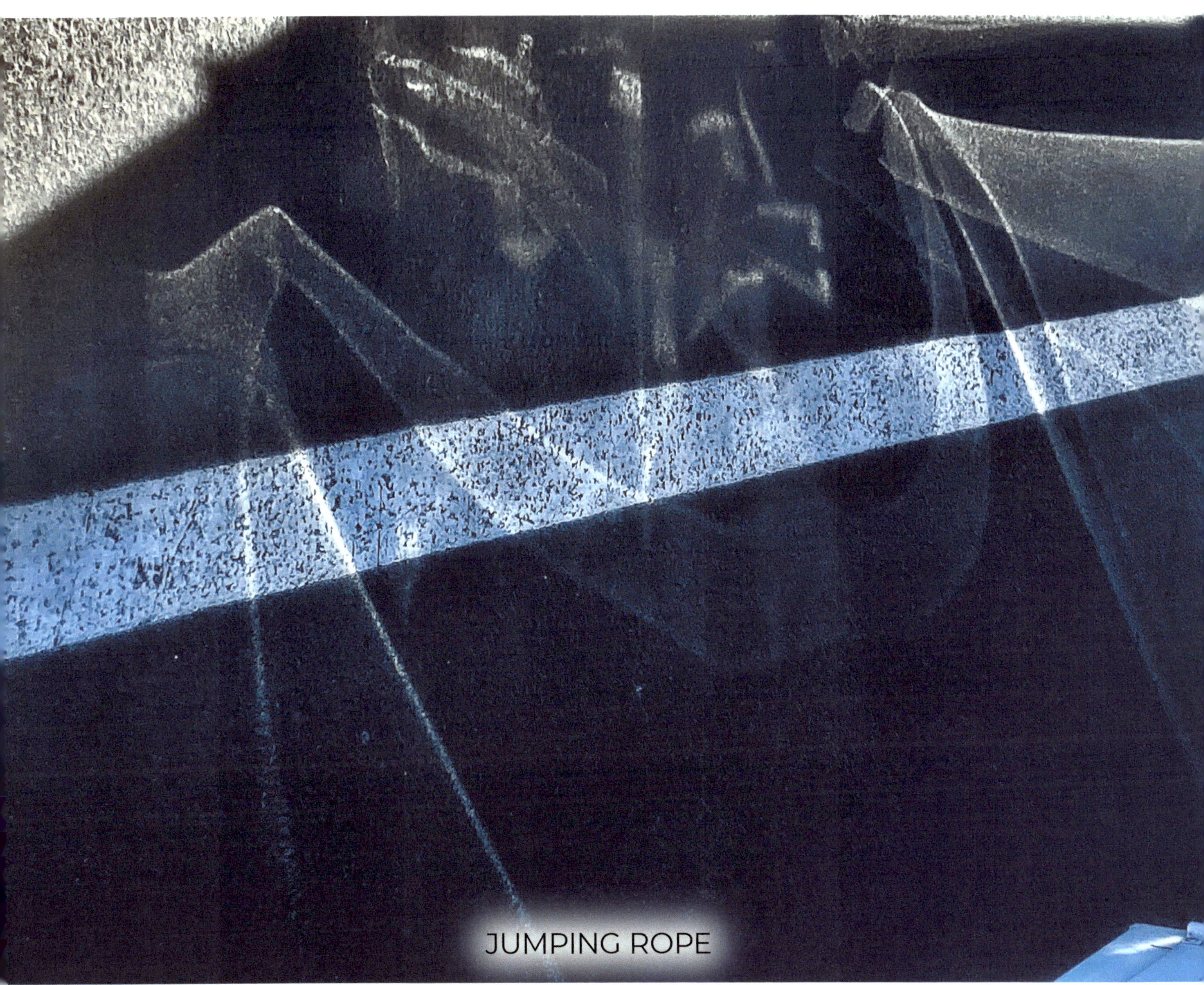

JUMPING ROPE

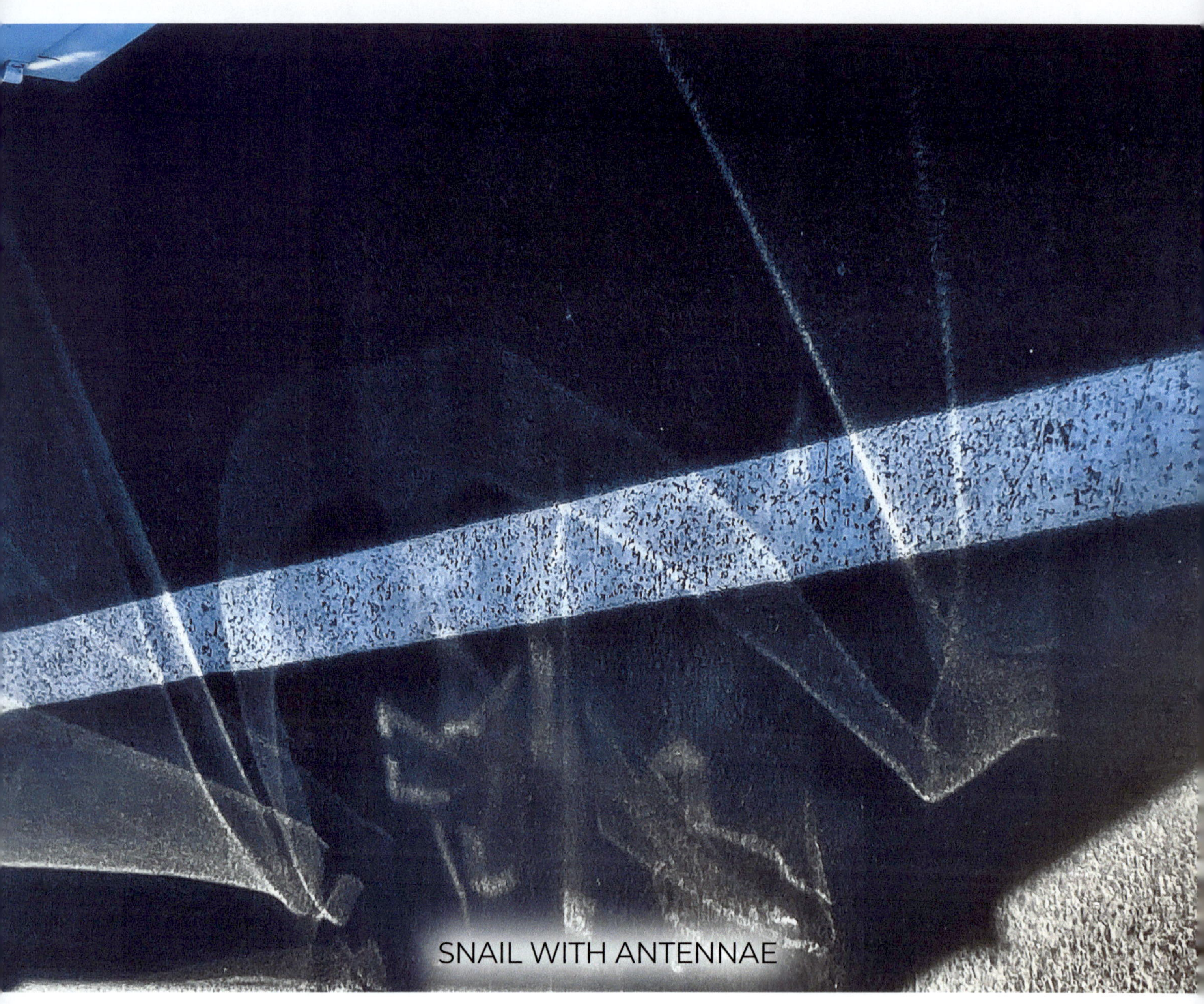

SNAIL WITH ANTENNAE

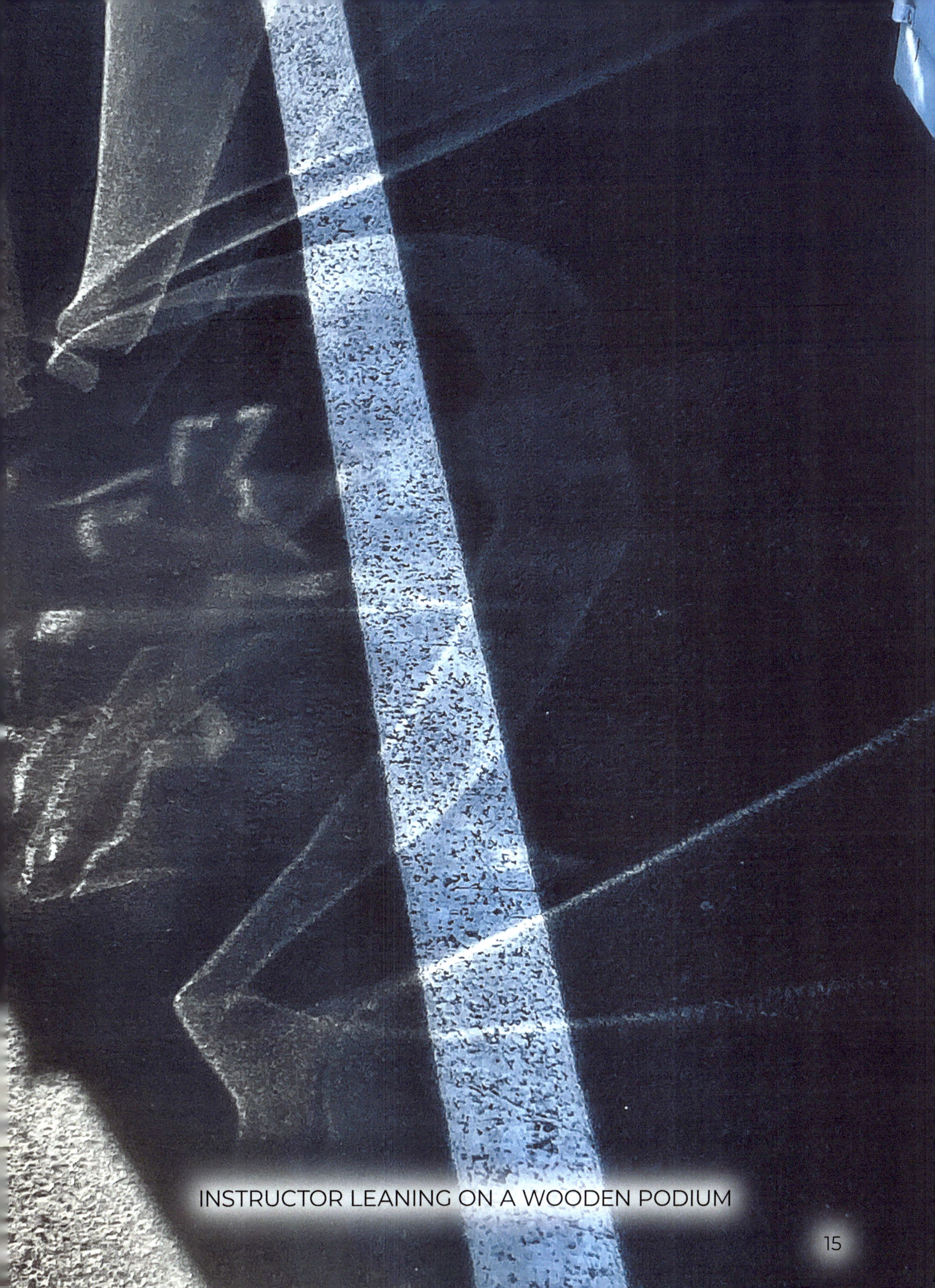

INSTRUCTOR LEANING ON A WOODEN PODIUM

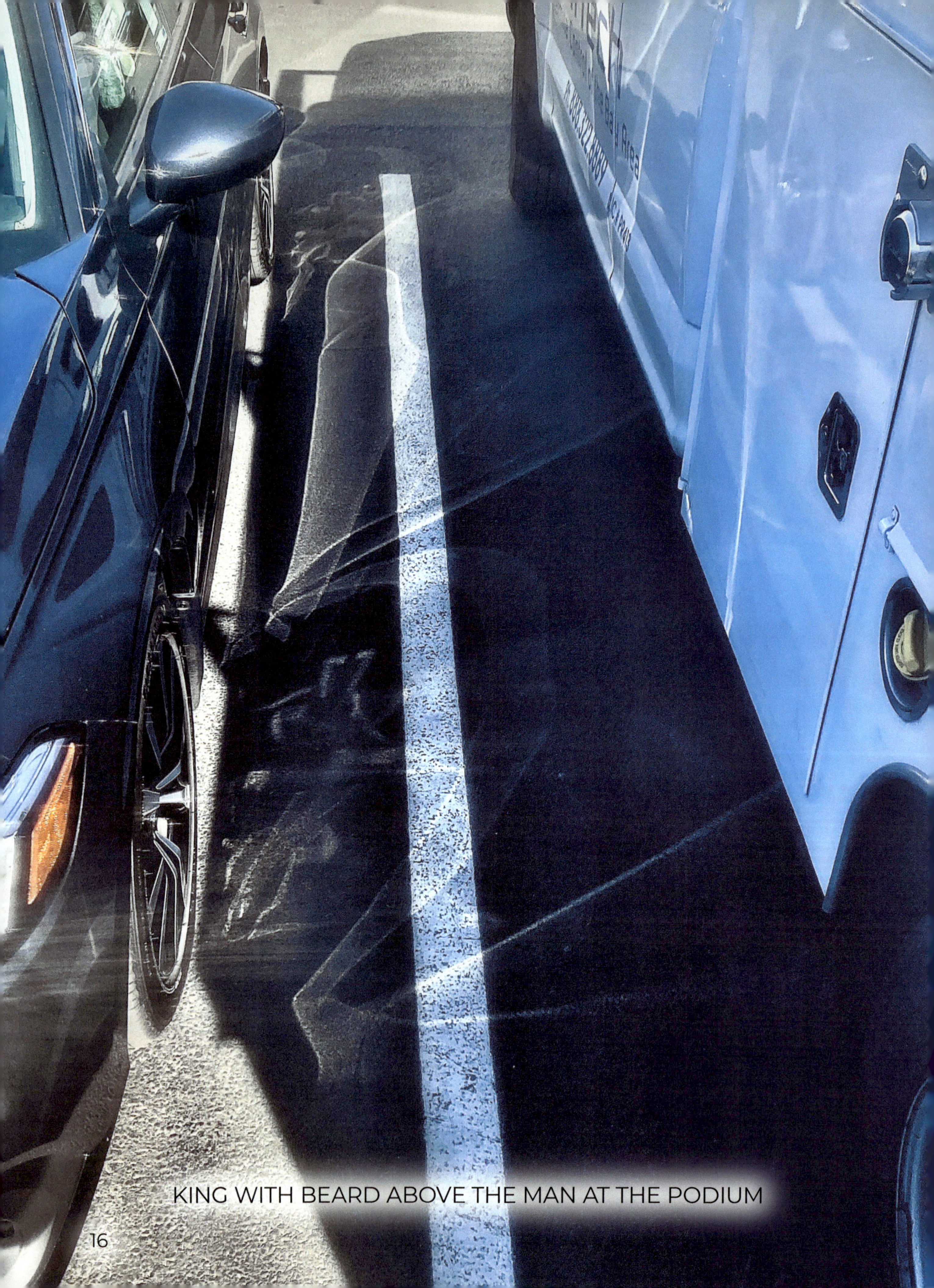

KING WITH BEARD ABOVE THE MAN AT THE PODIUM

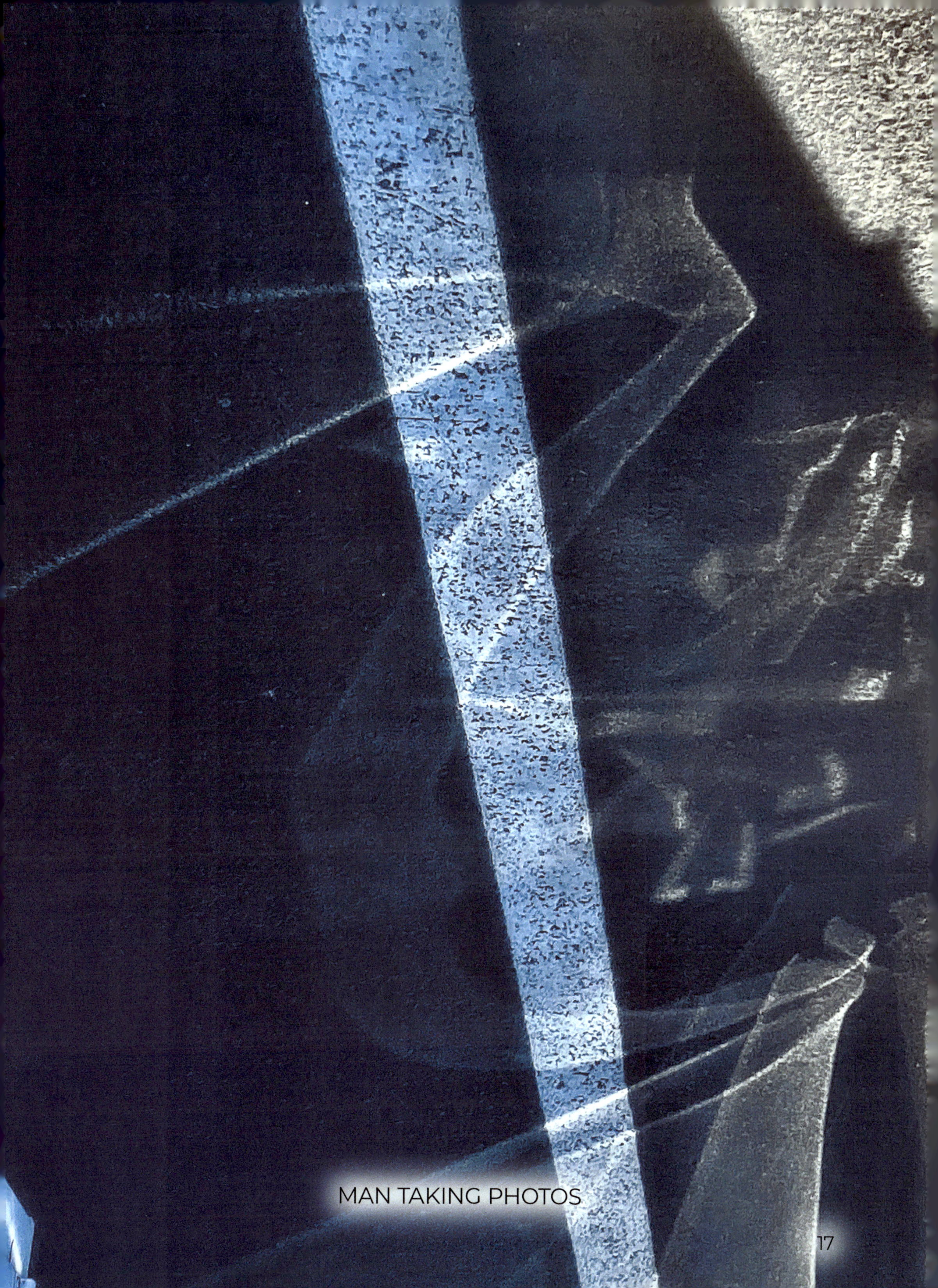
MAN TAKING PHOTOS

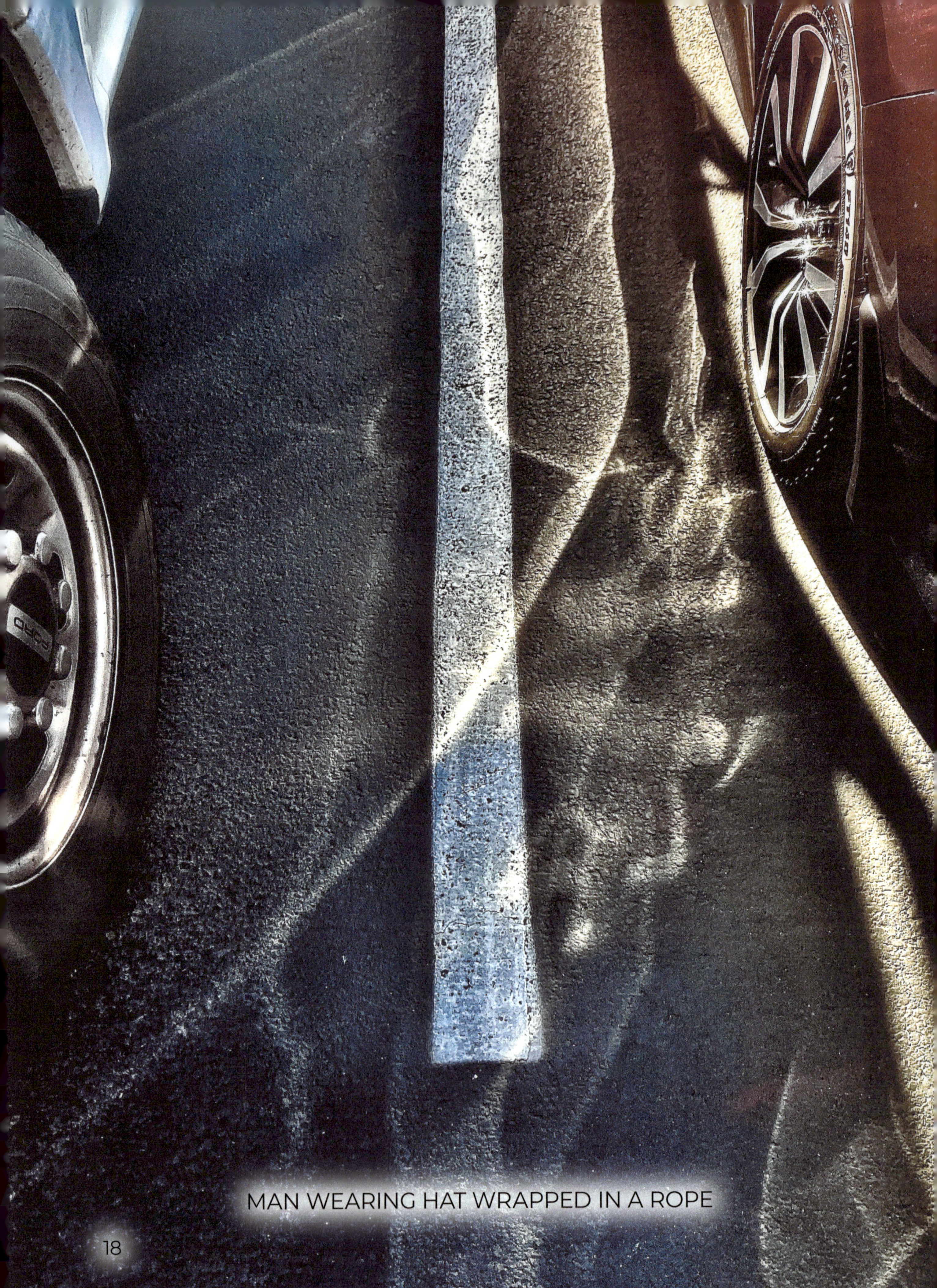

MAN WEARING HAT WRAPPED IN A ROPE

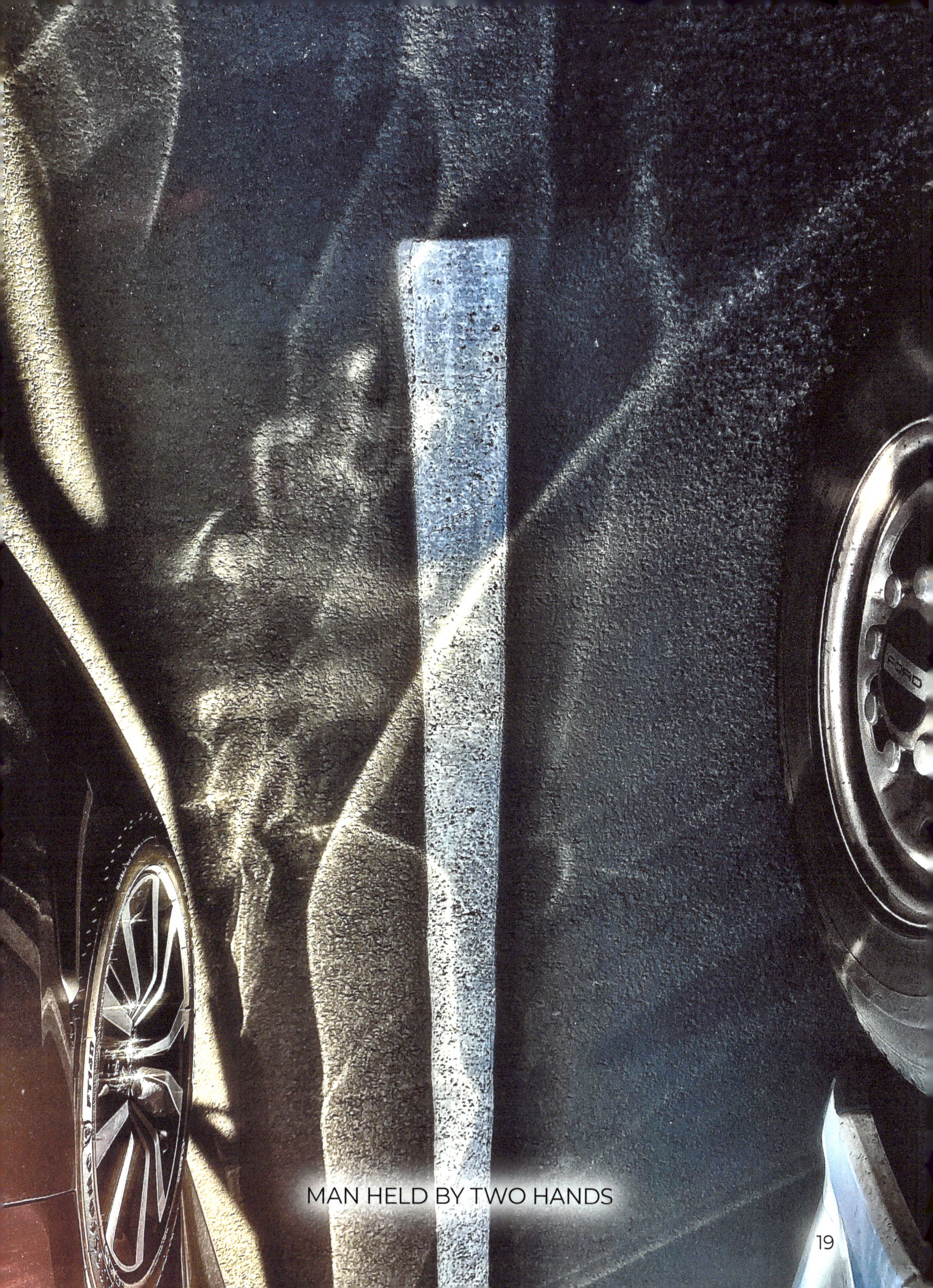

MAN HELD BY TWO HANDS

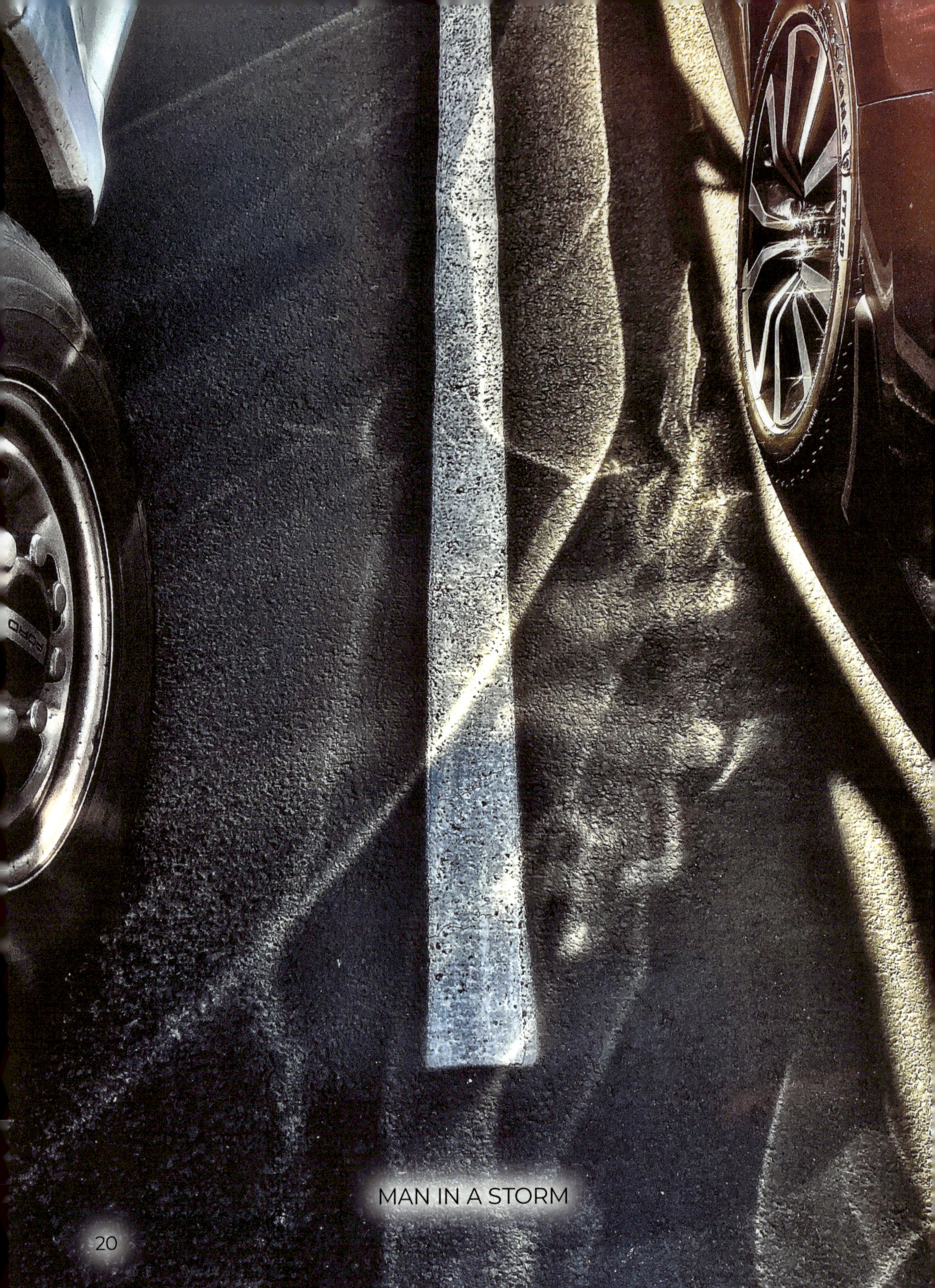

MAN IN A STORM

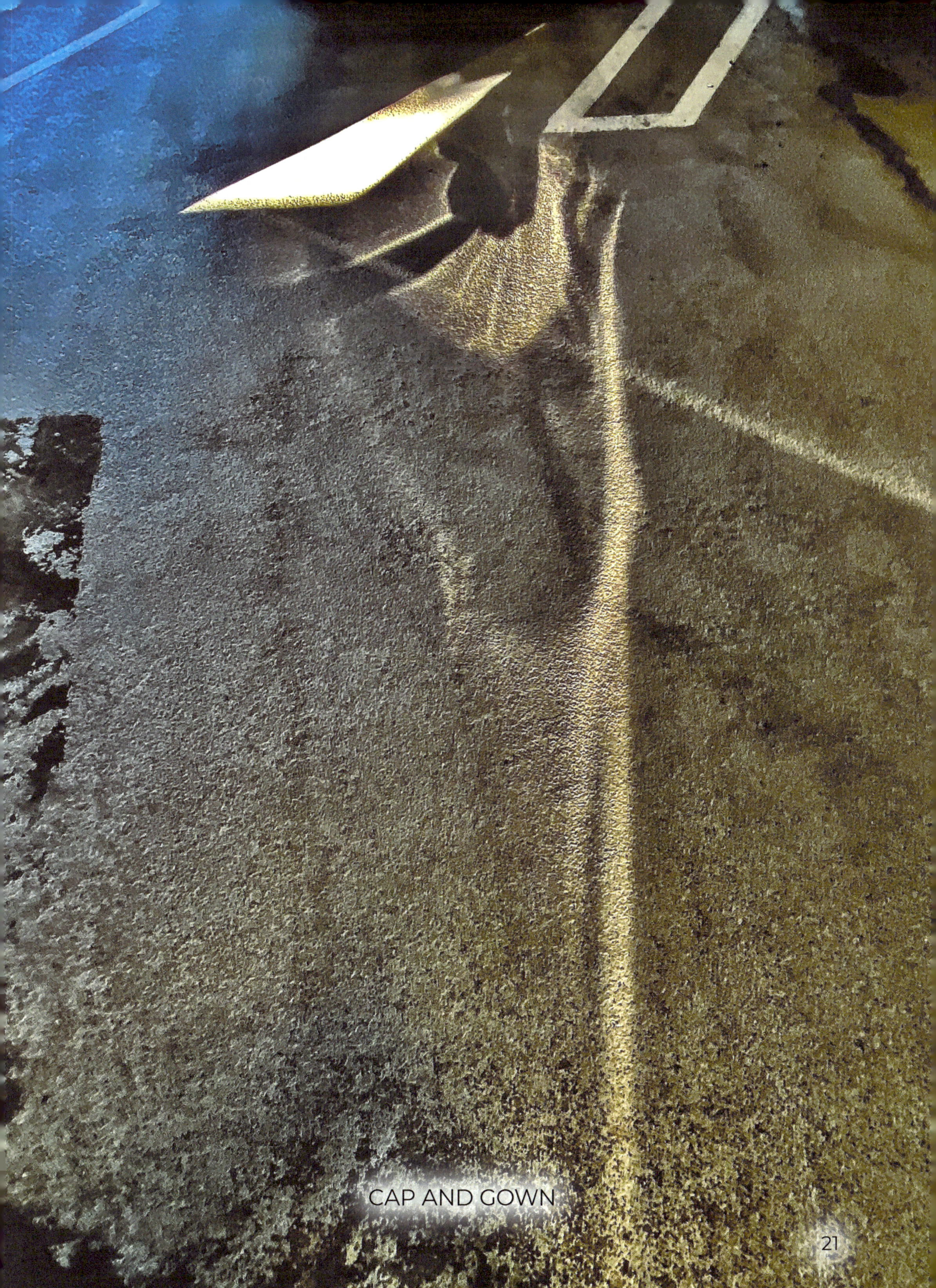

CAP AND GOWN

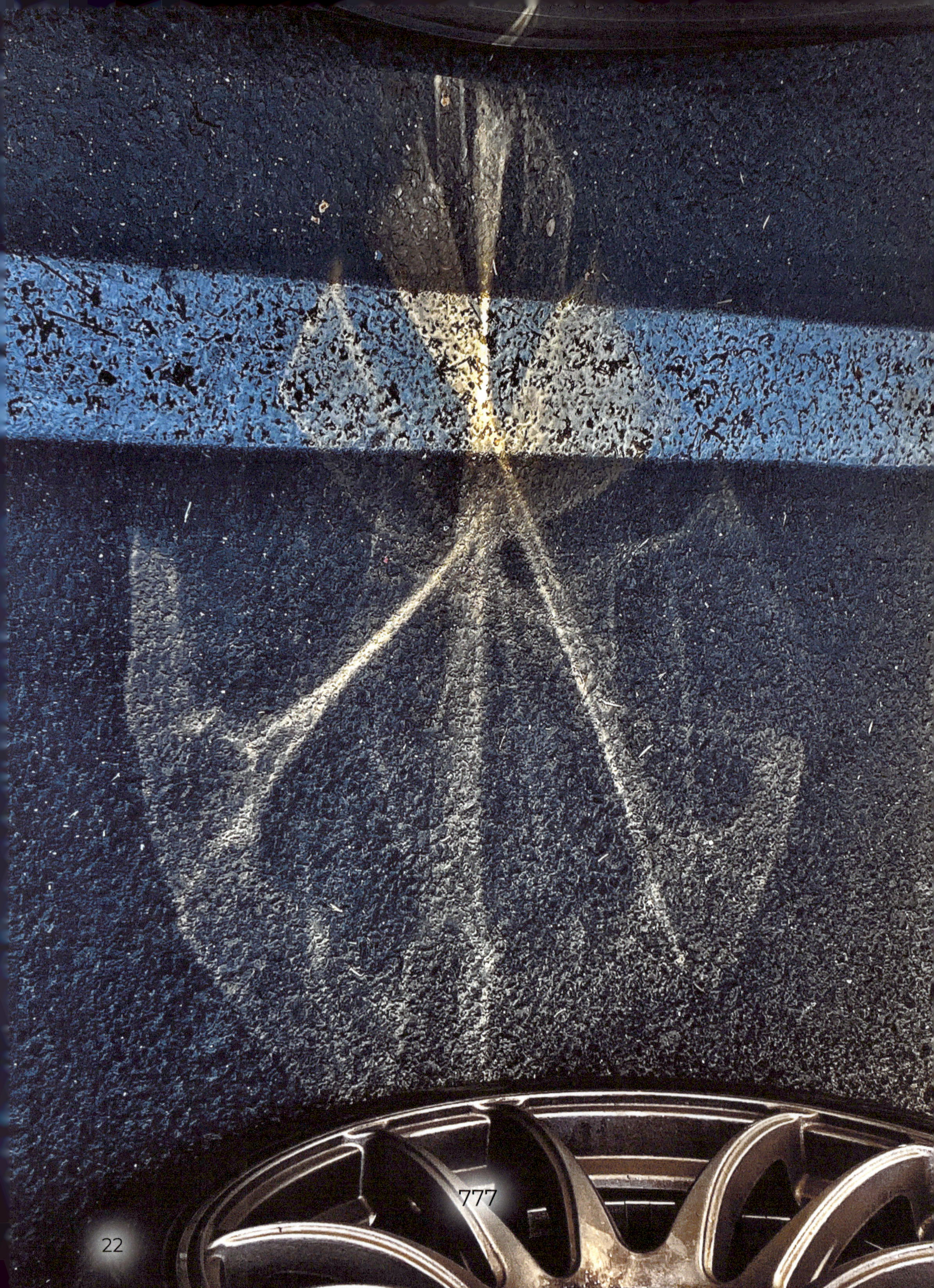

777

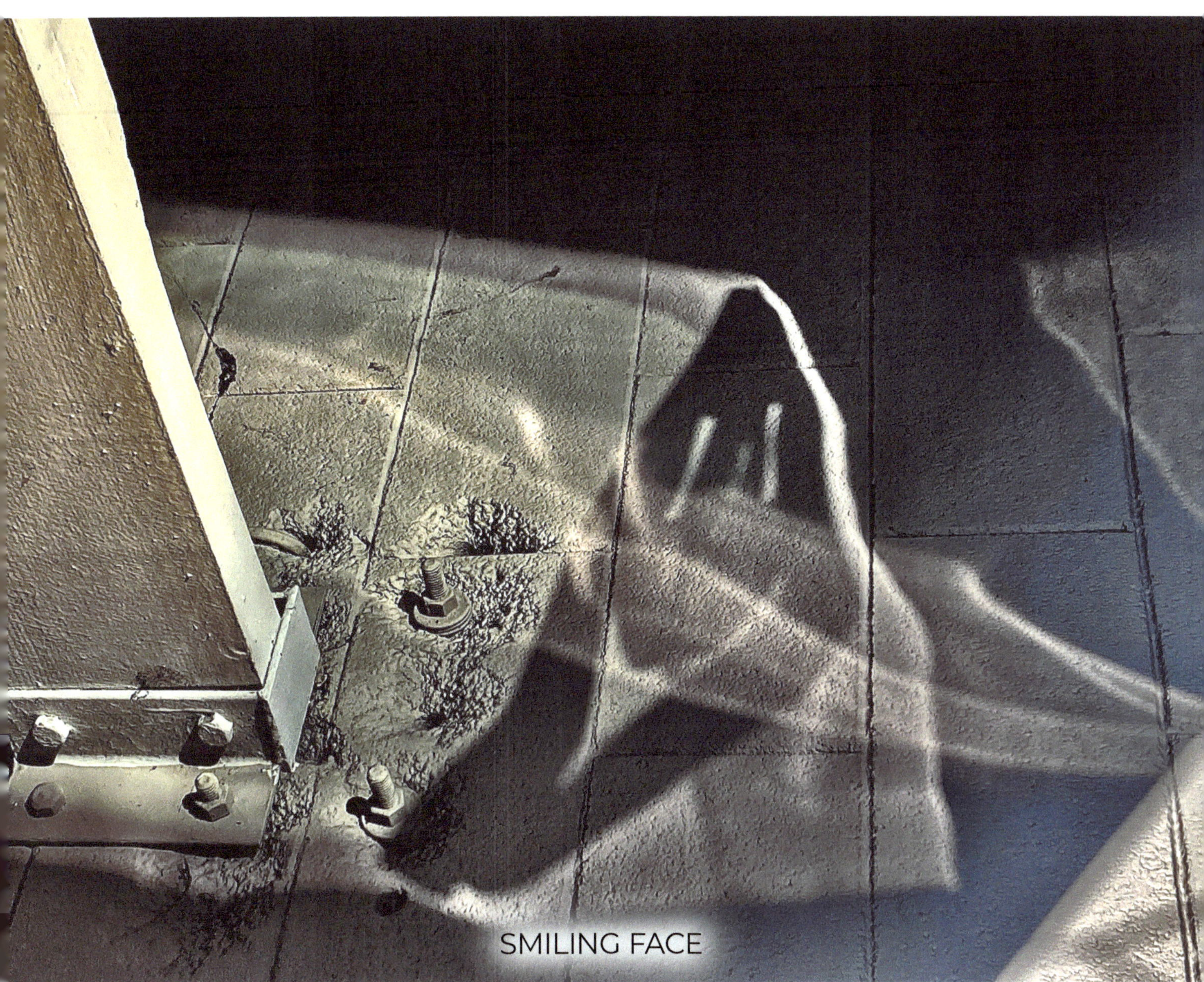

SMILING FACE

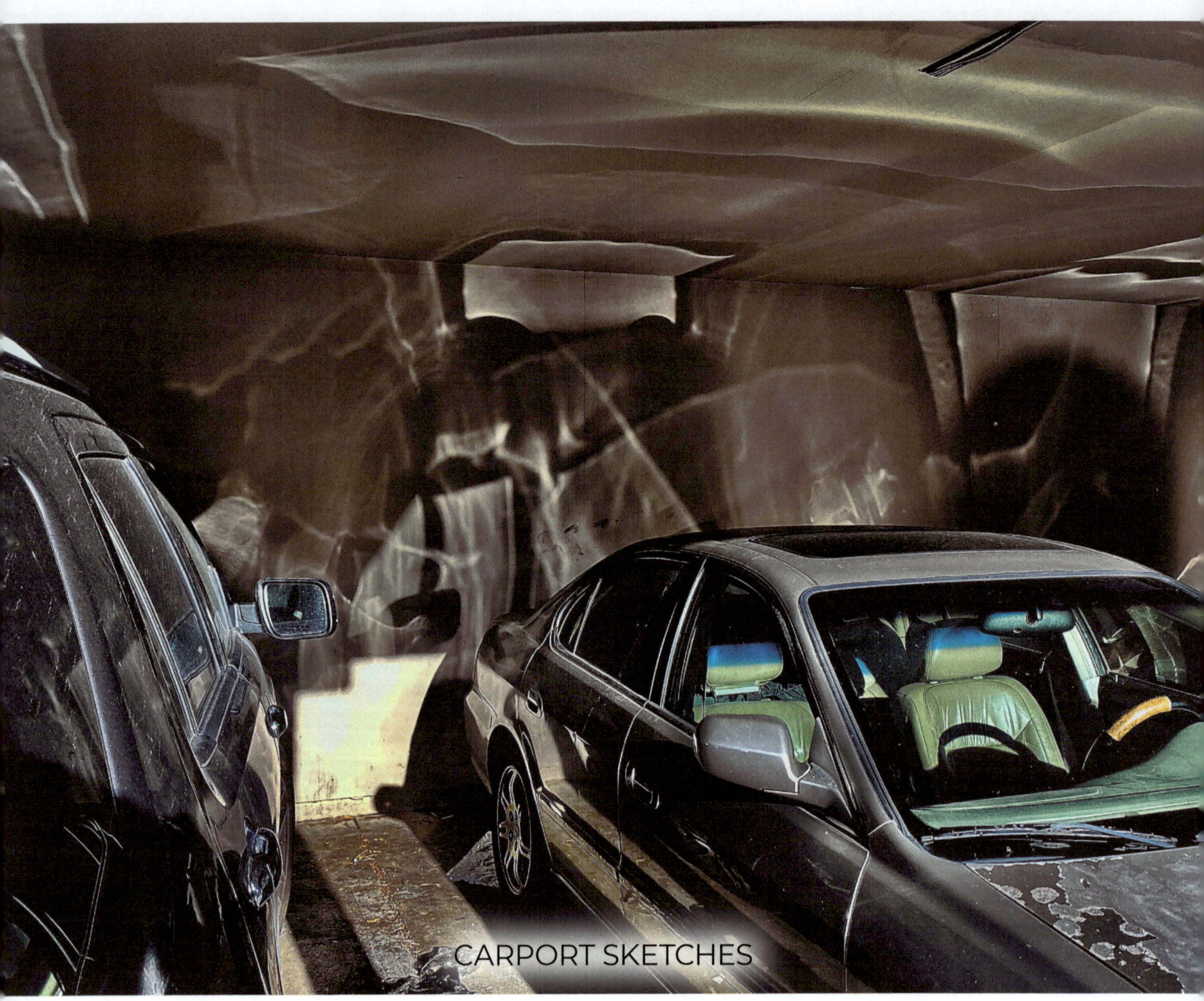

CARPORT SKETCHES

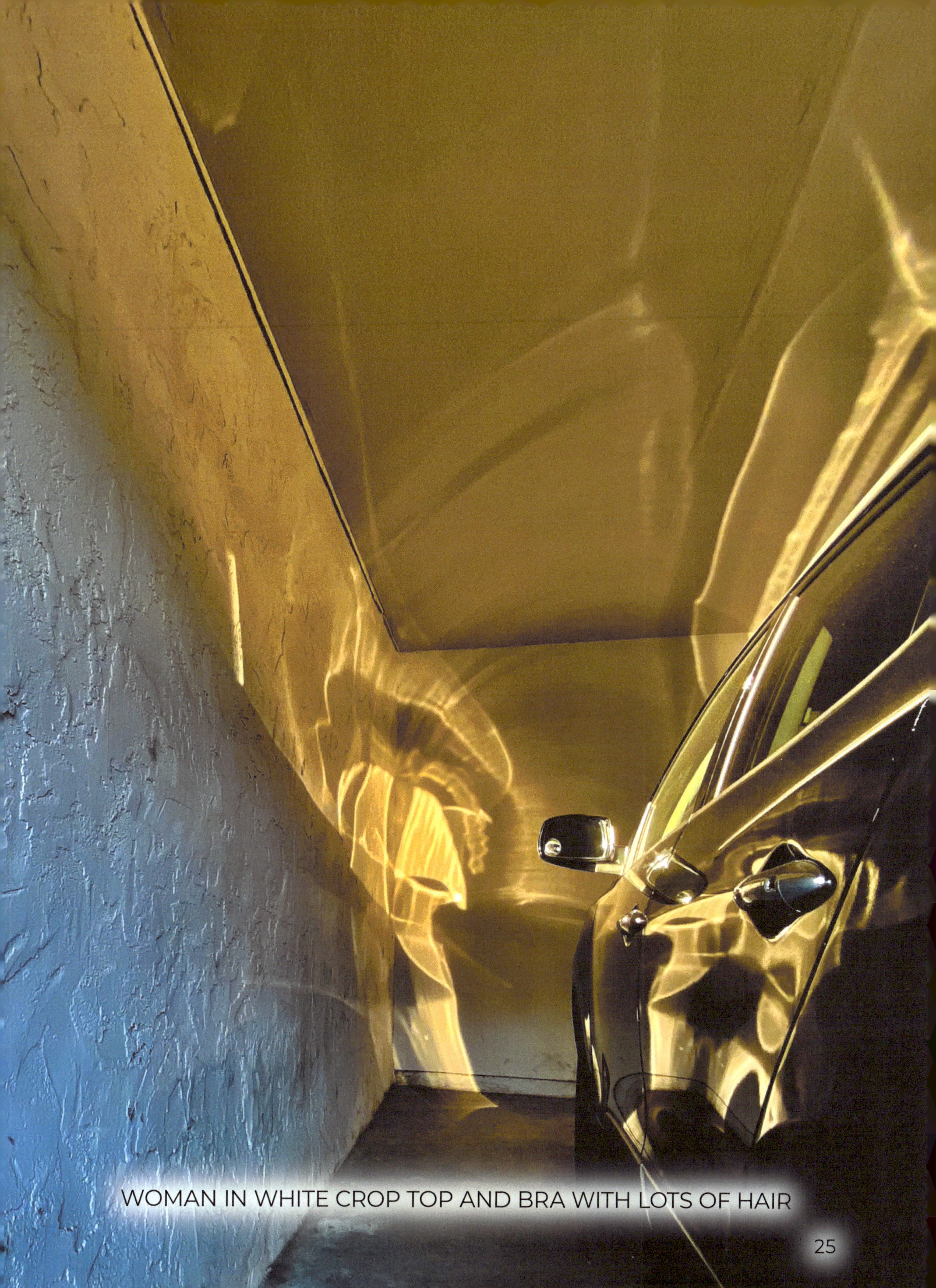

WOMAN IN WHITE CROP TOP AND BRA WITH LOTS OF HAIR

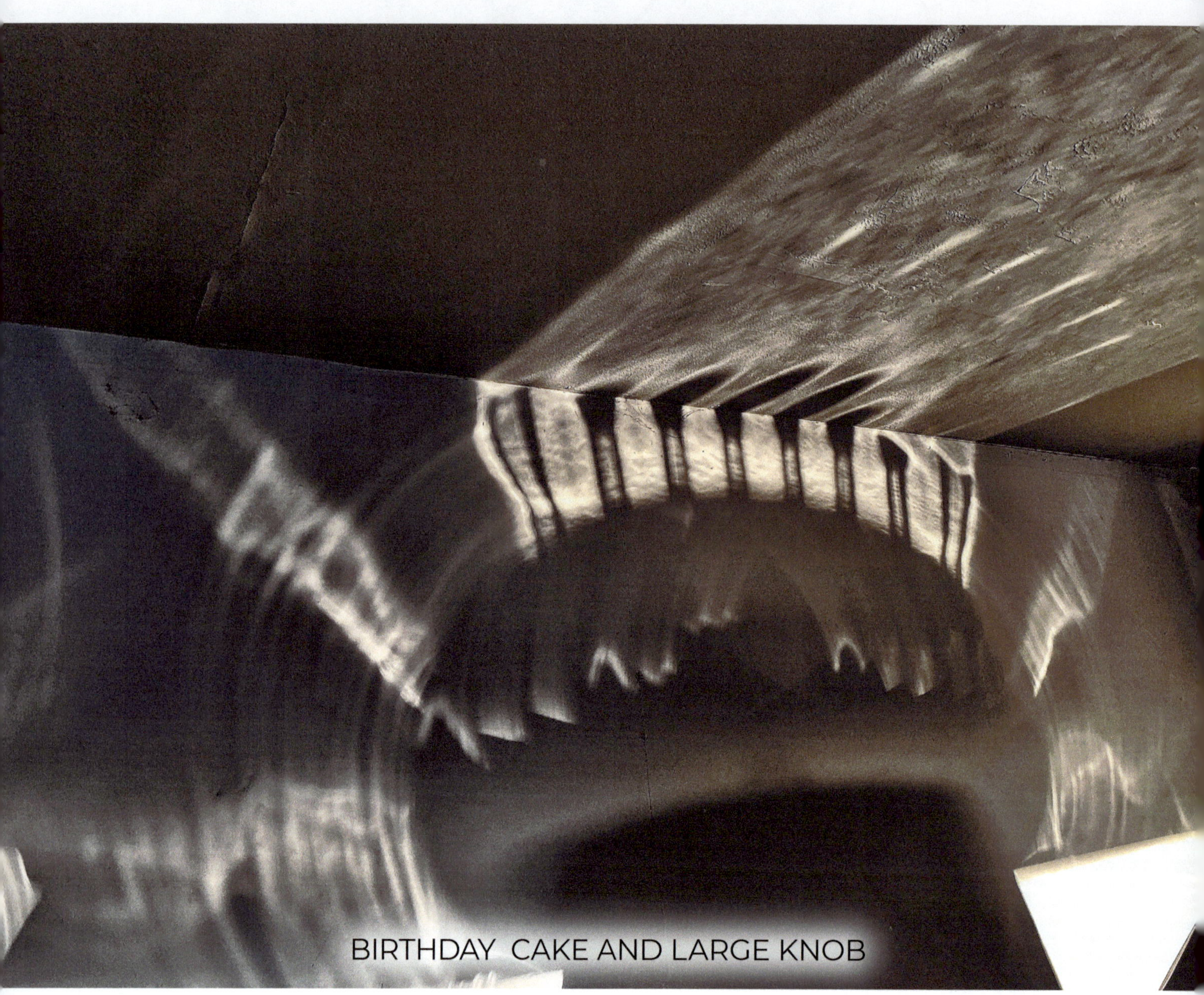

BIRTHDAY CAKE AND LARGE KNOB

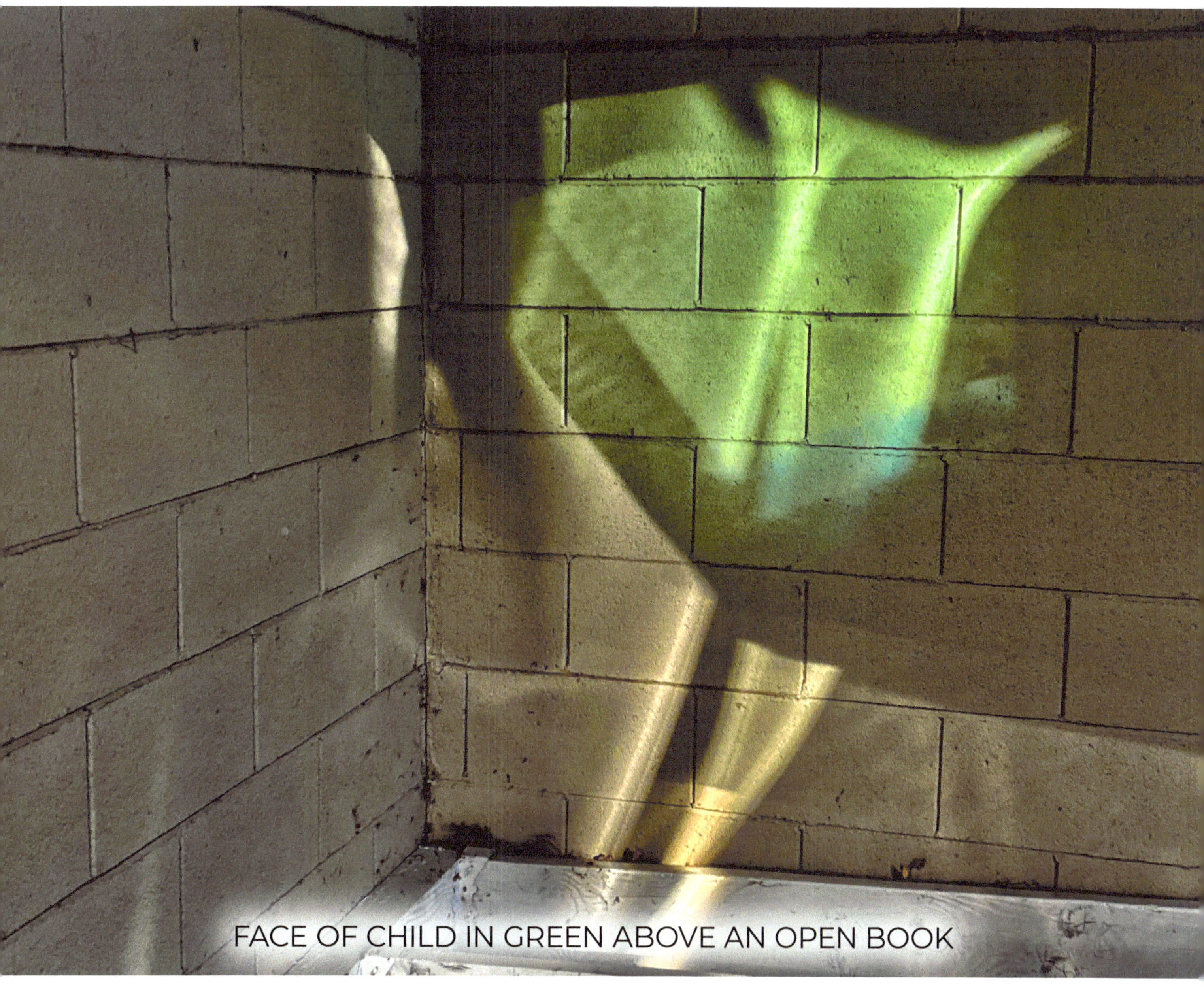

FACE OF CHILD IN GREEN ABOVE AN OPEN BOOK

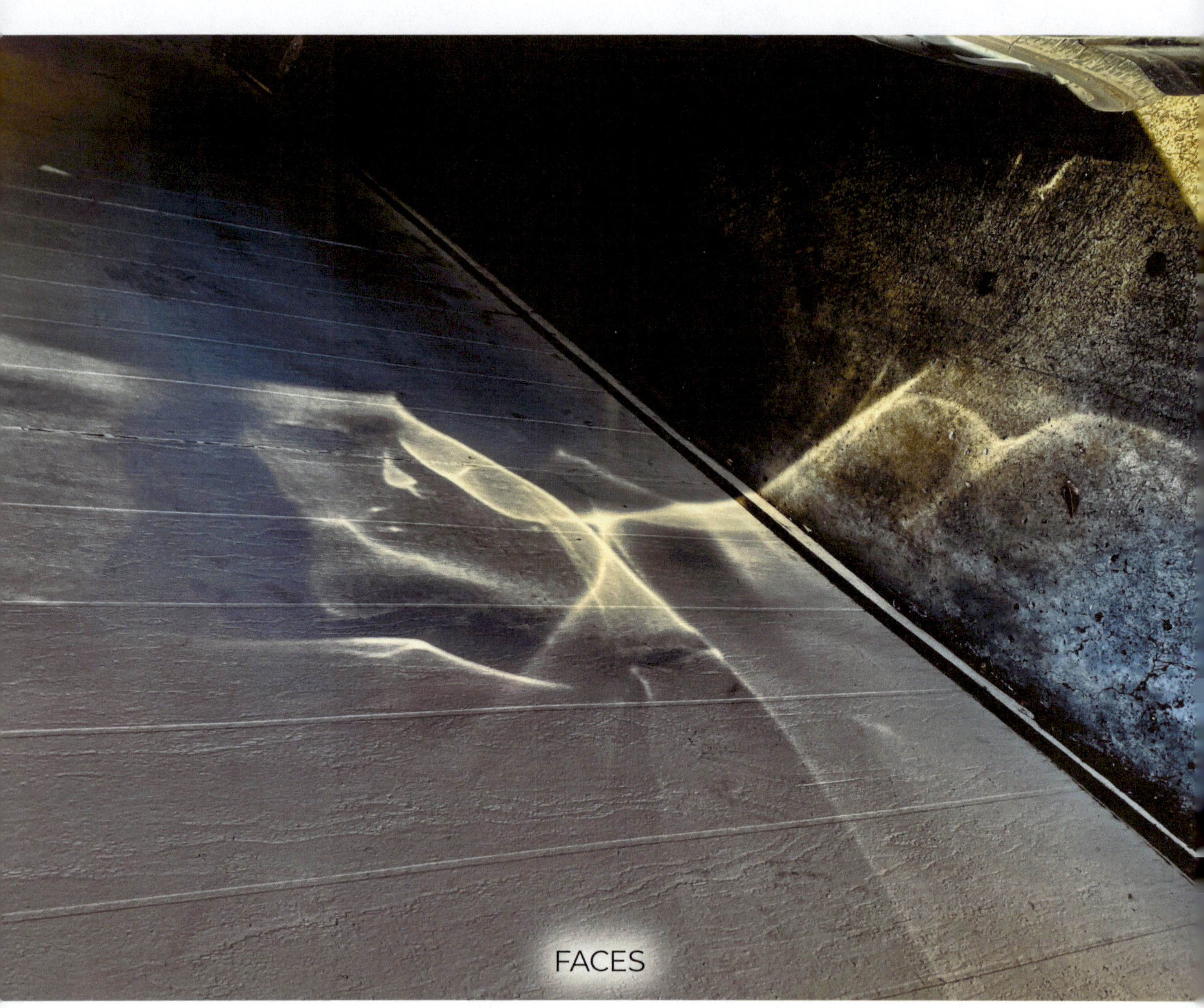
FACES

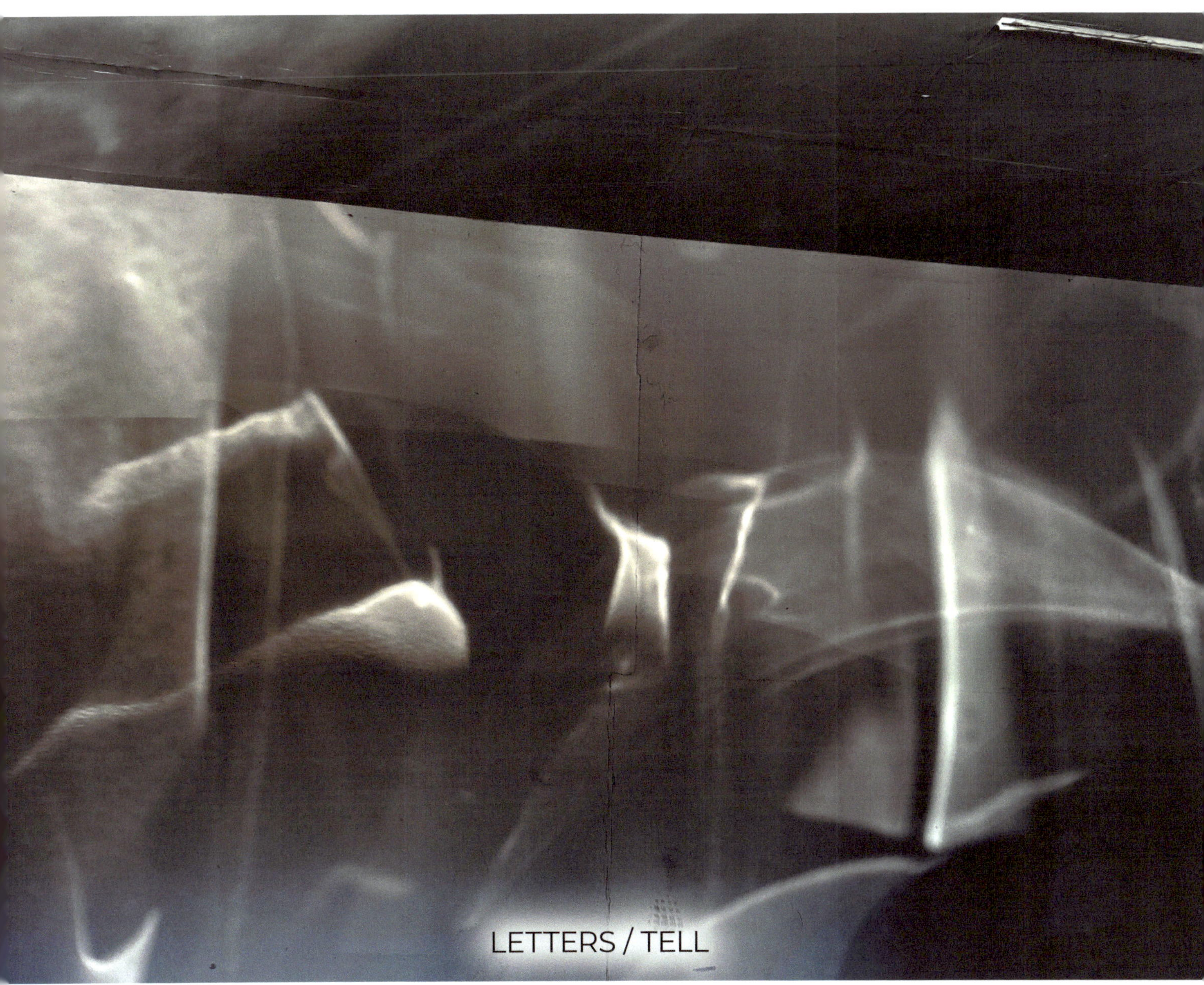

LETTERS / TELL

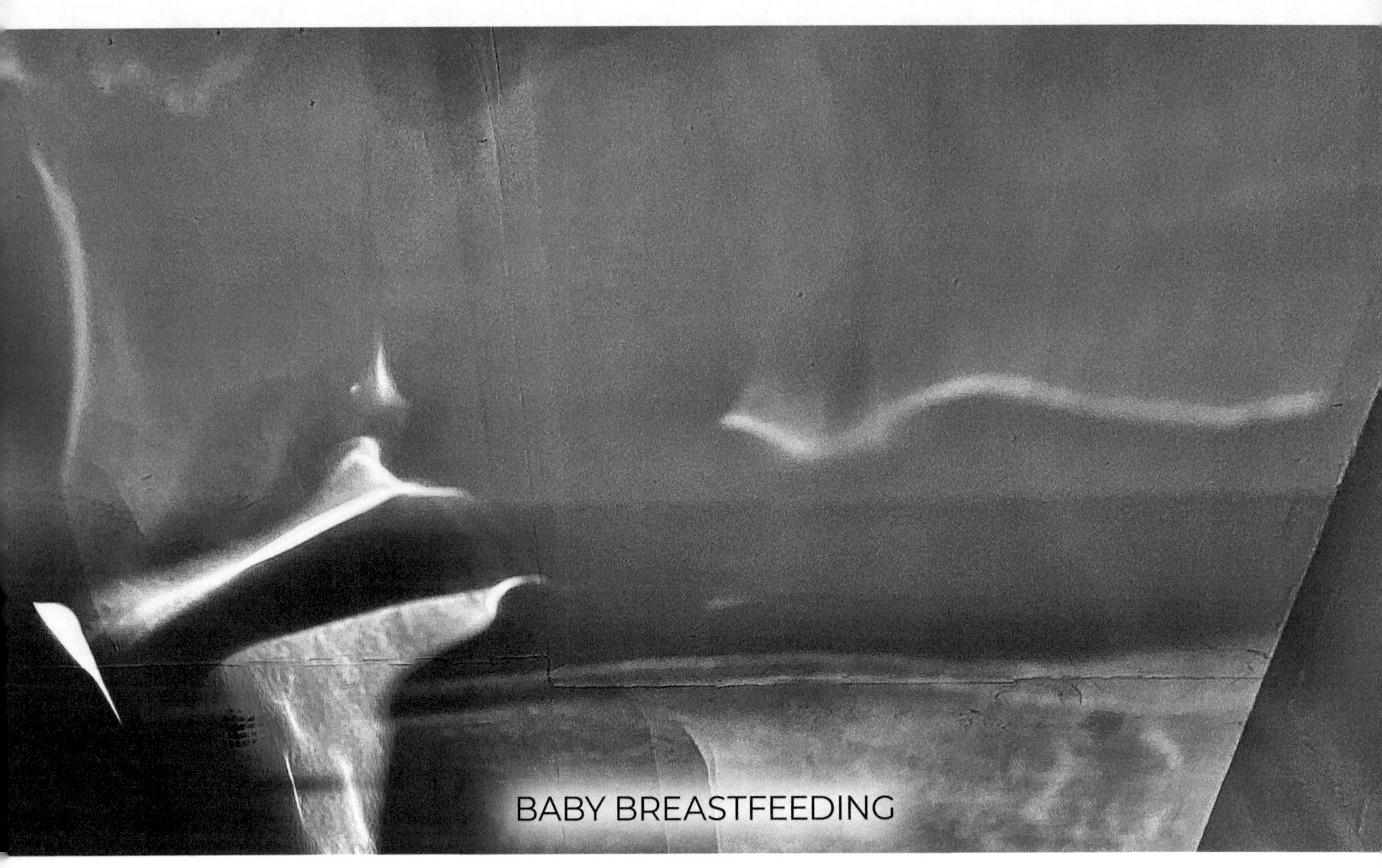

BABY BREASTFEEDING

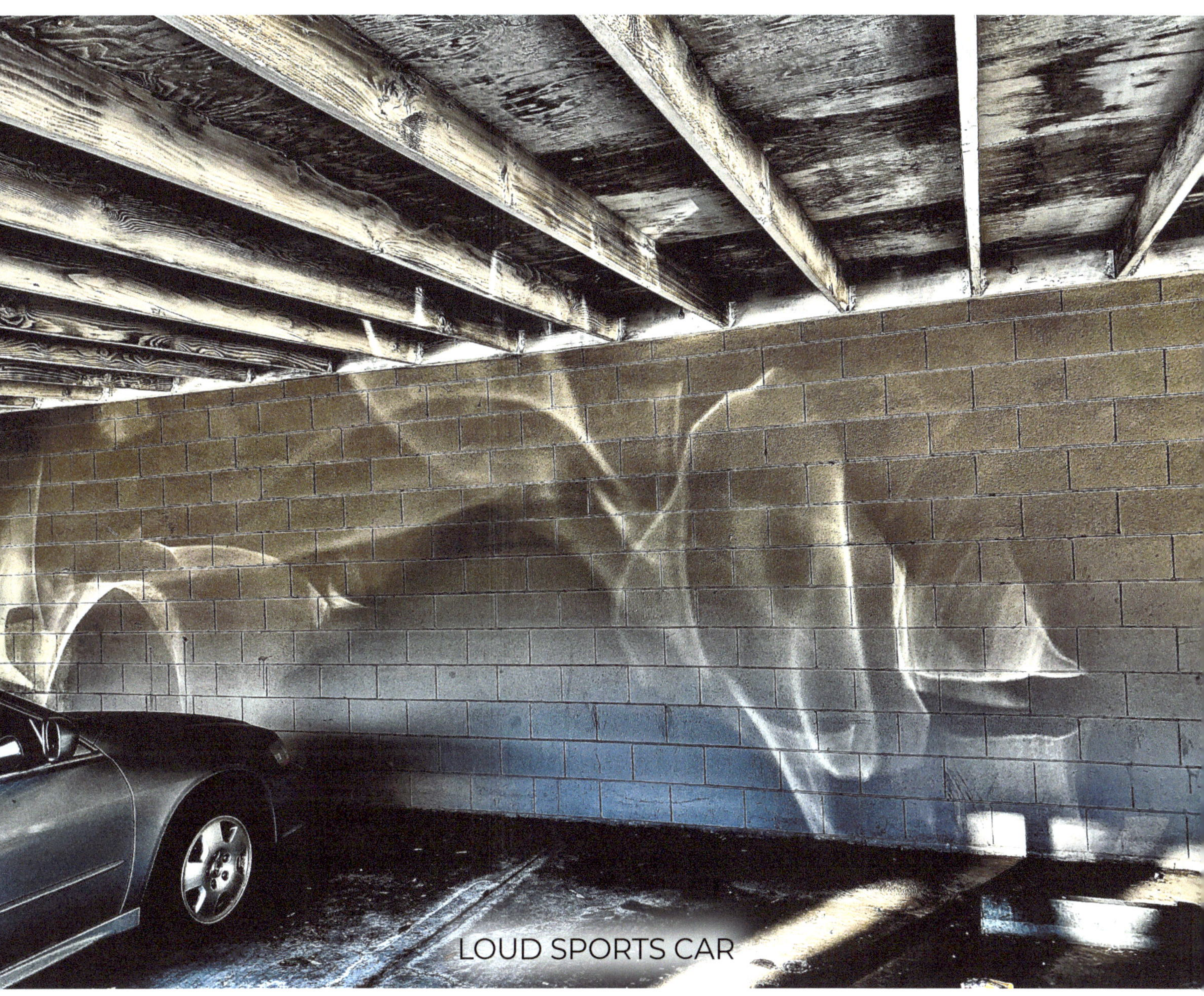

LOUD SPORTS CAR

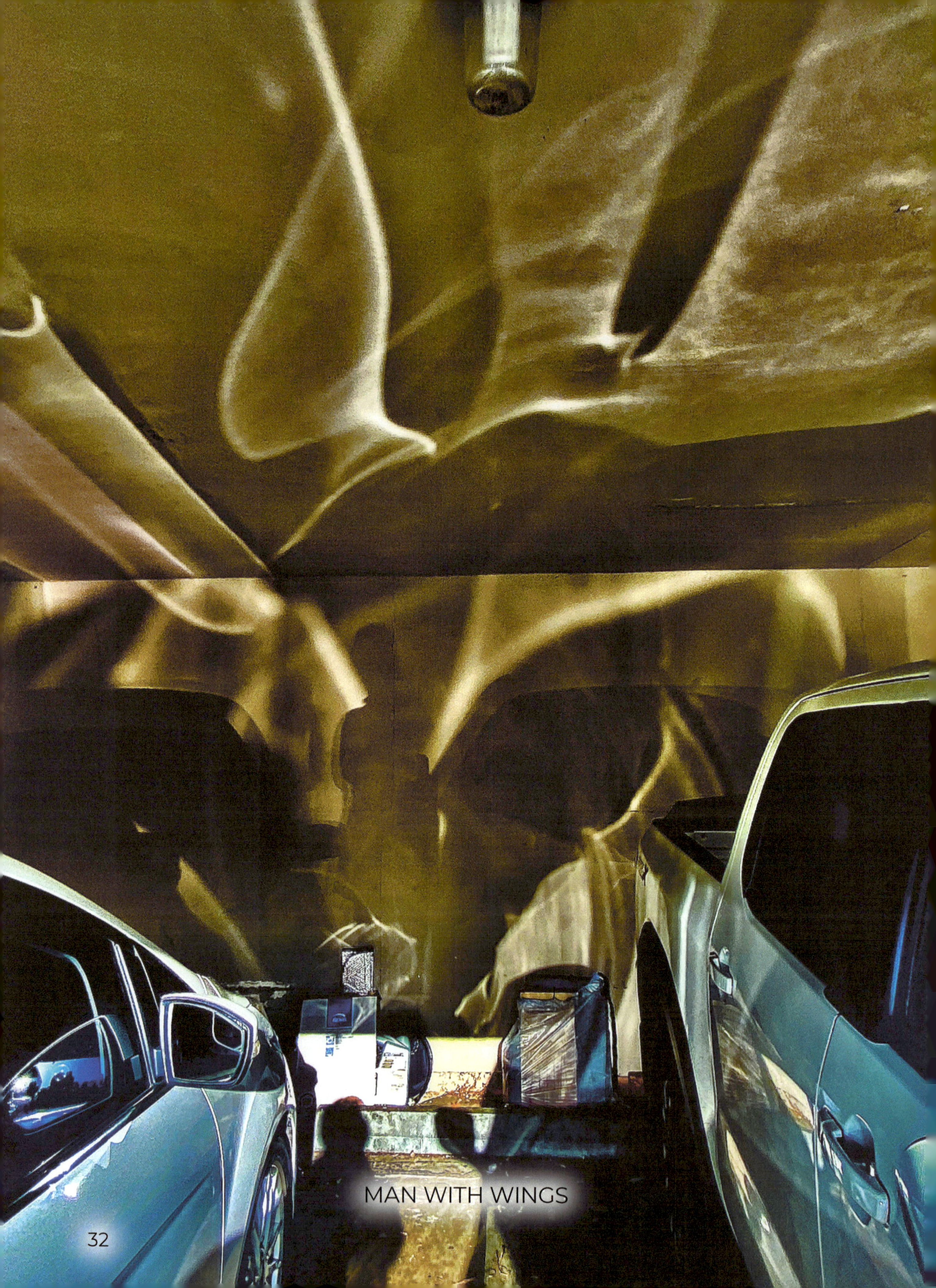

MAN WITH WINGS

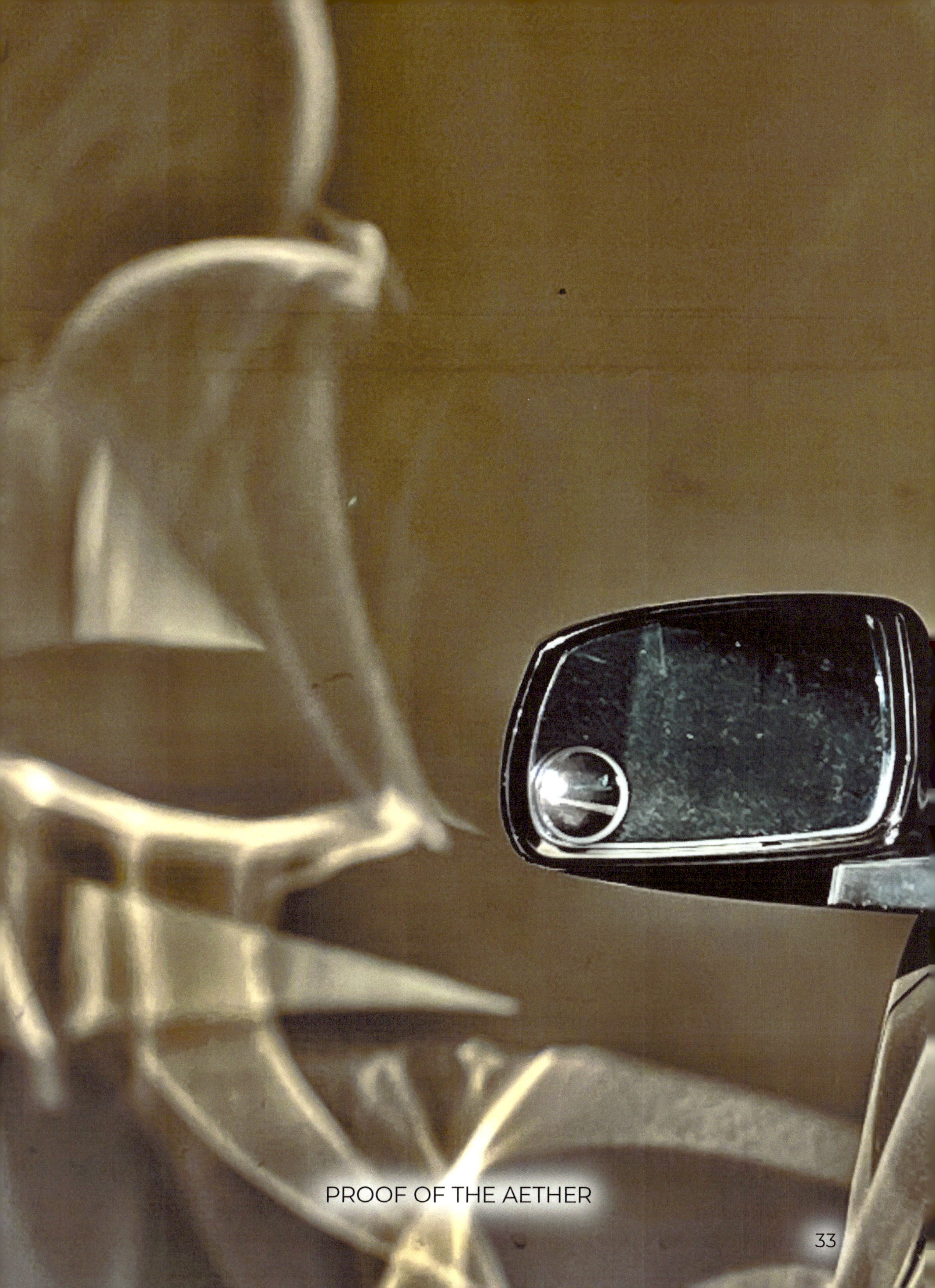

PROOF OF THE AETHER

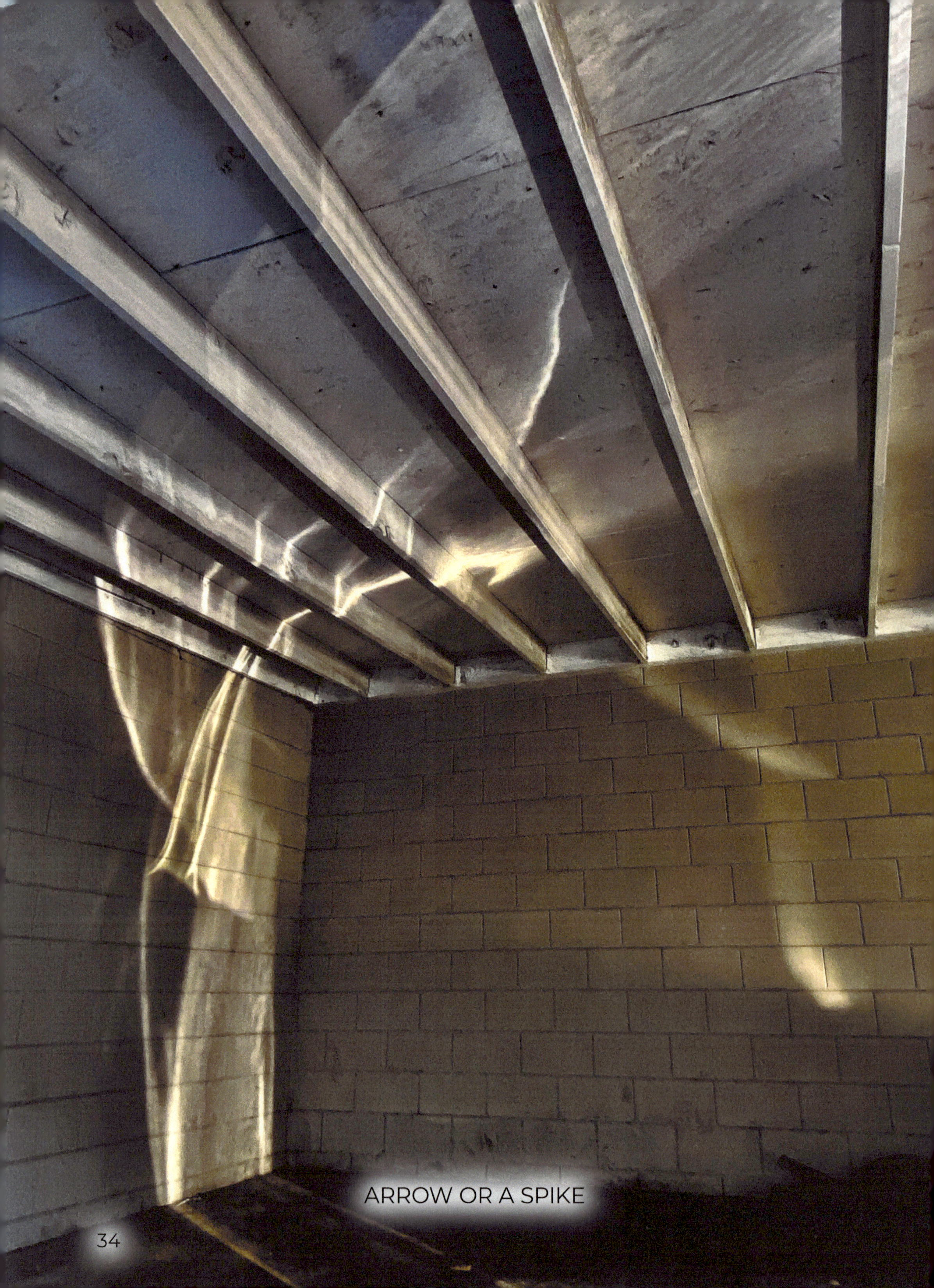

ARROW OR A SPIKE

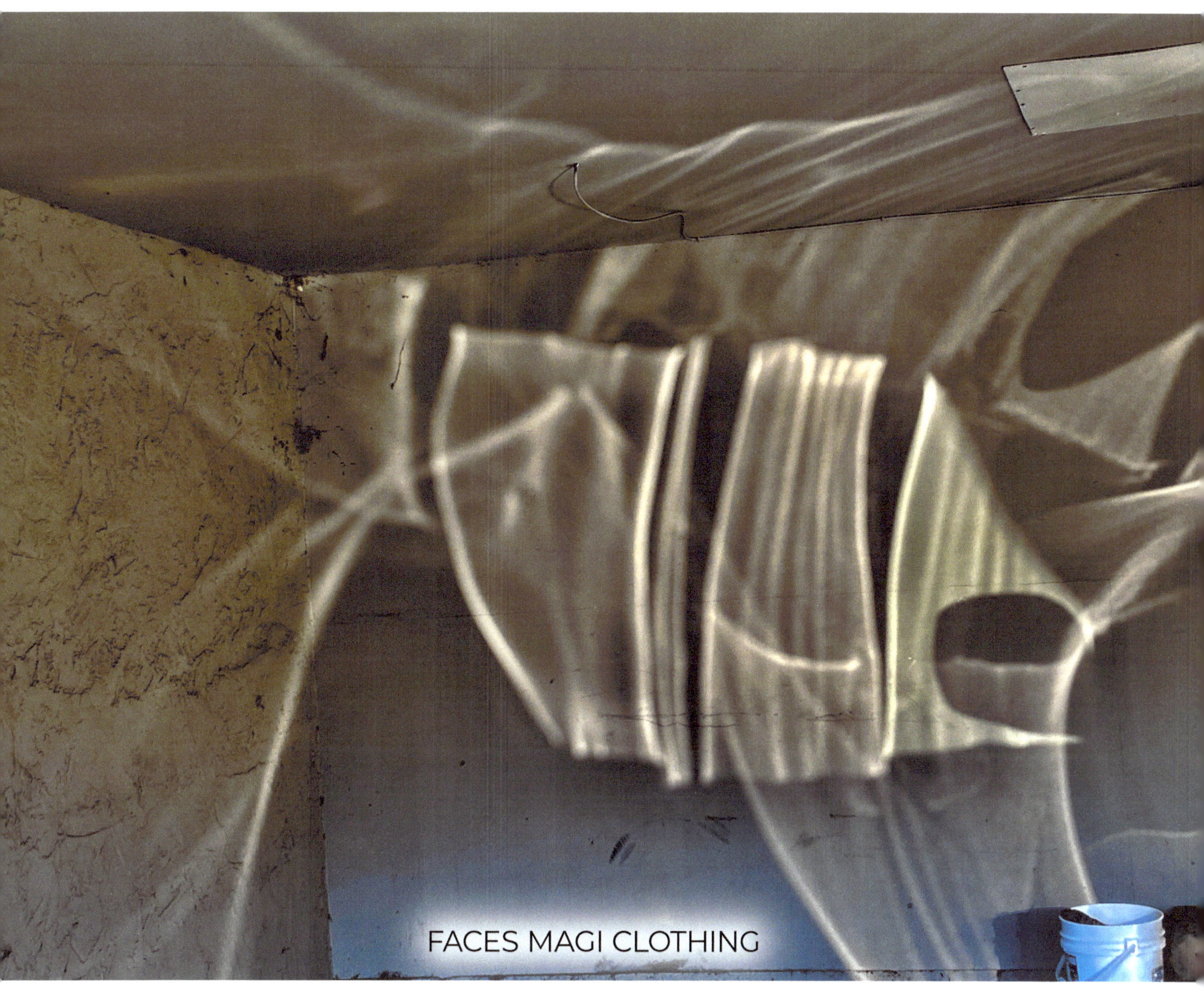
FACES MAGI CLOTHING

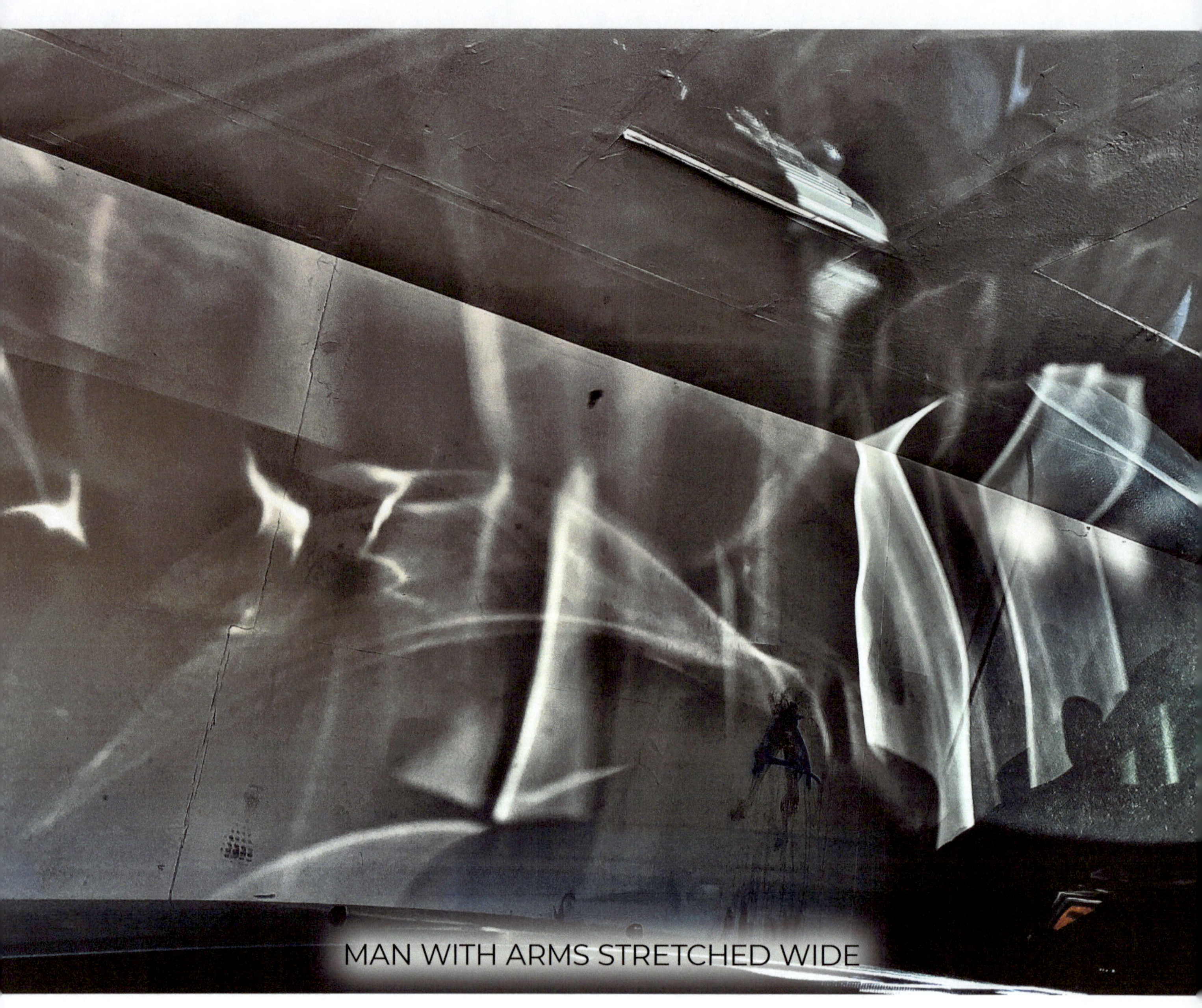
MAN WITH ARMS STRETCHED WIDE

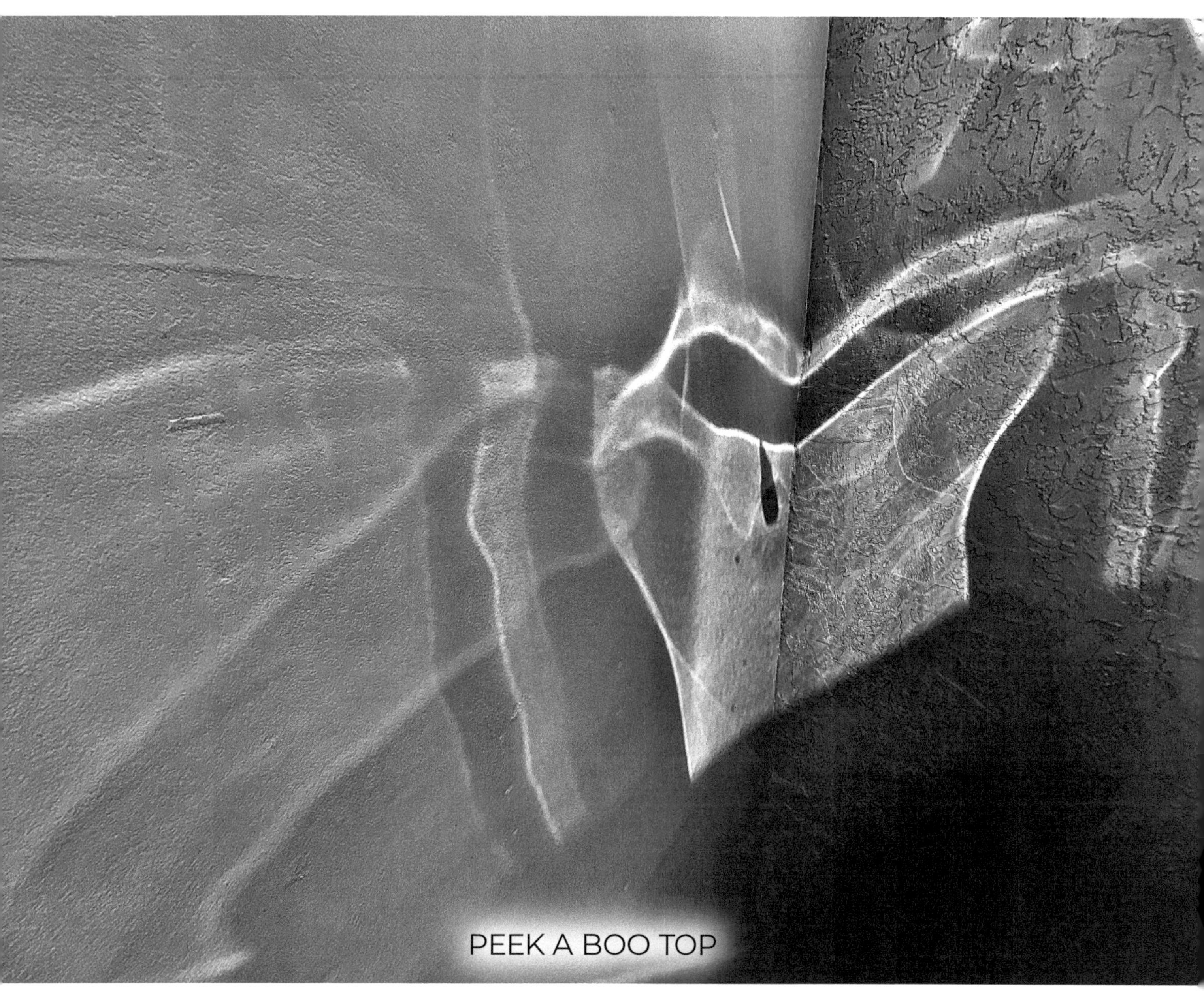

PEEK A BOO TOP

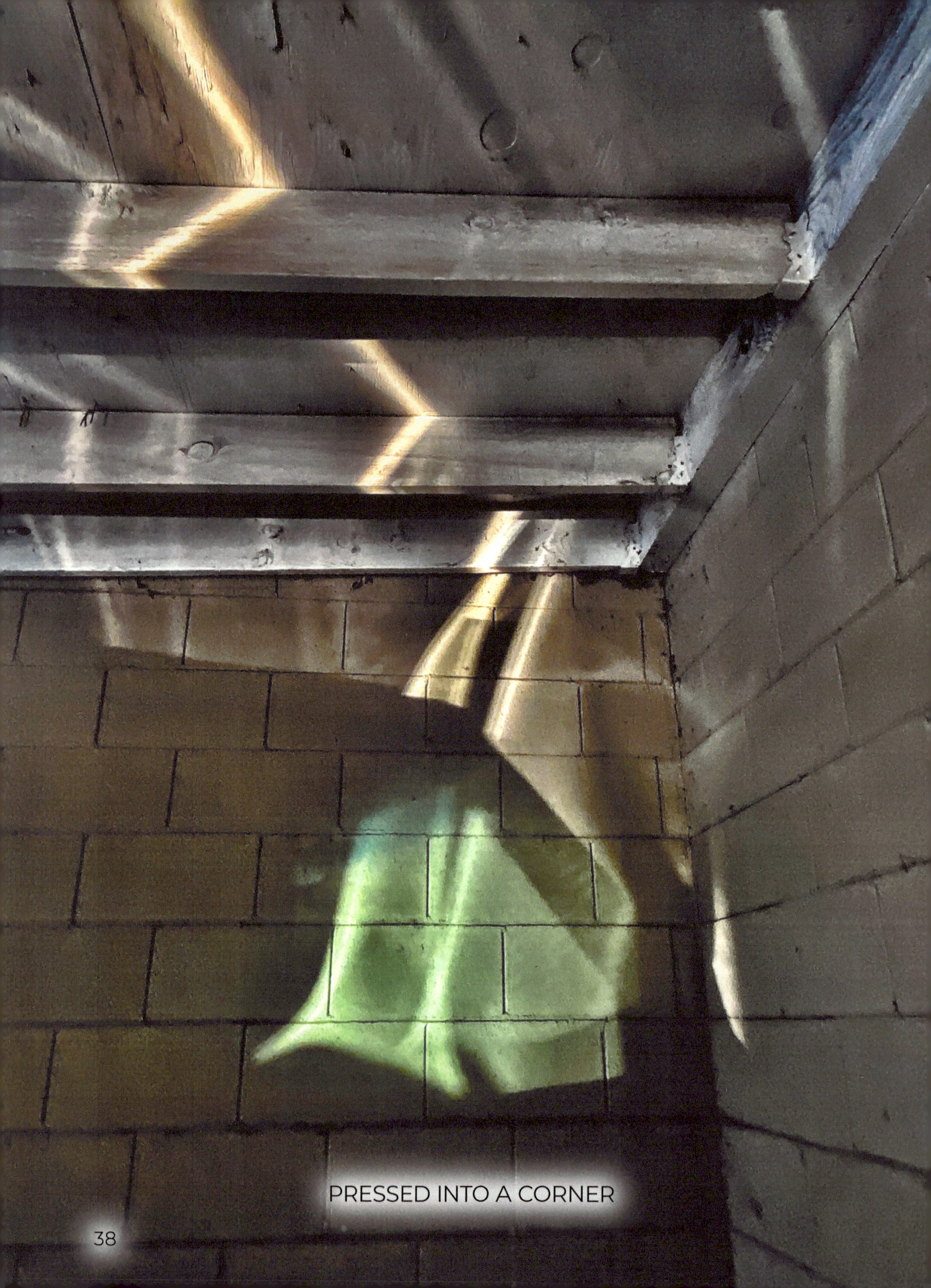

PRESSED INTO A CORNER

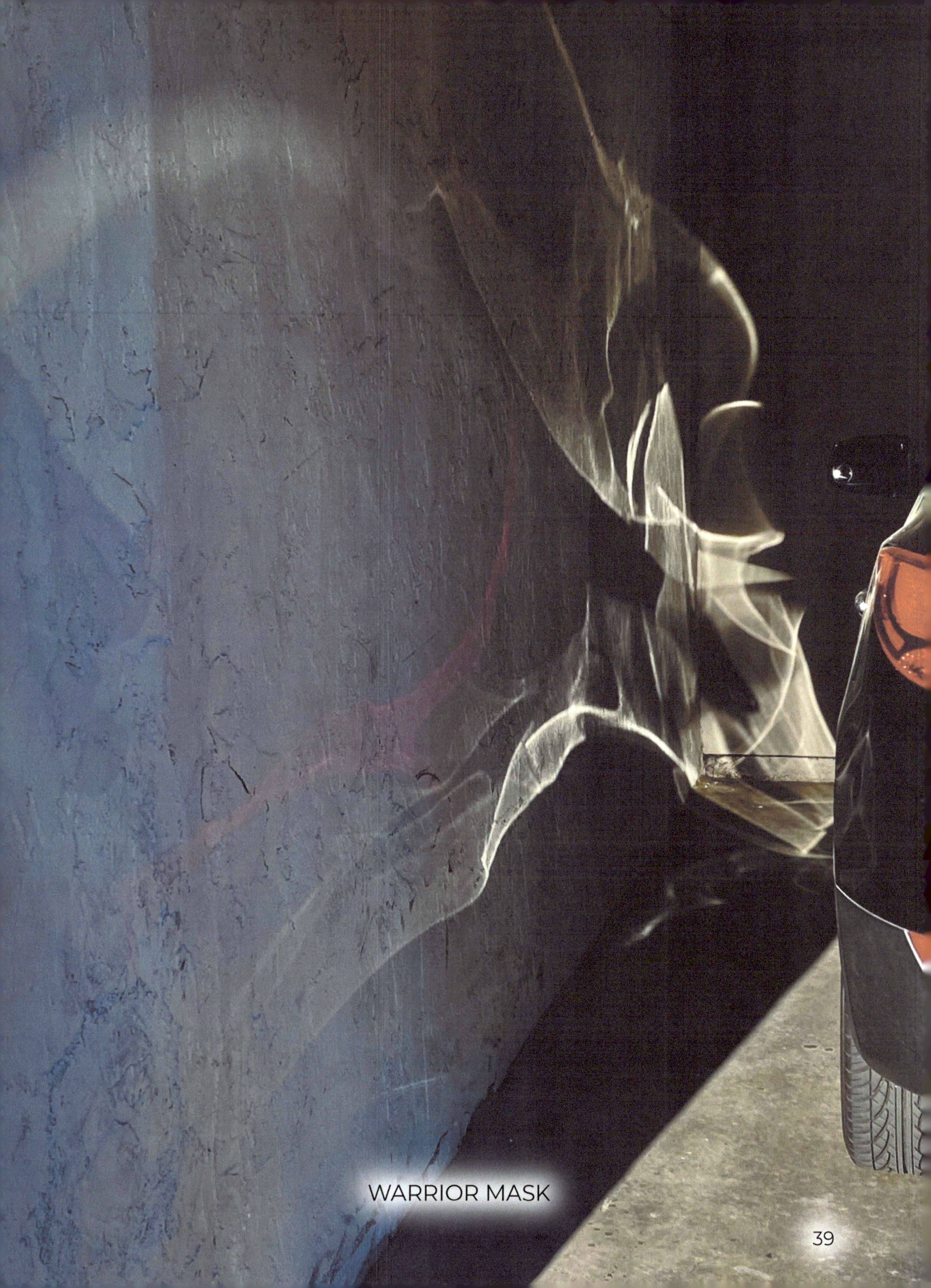

WARRIOR MASK

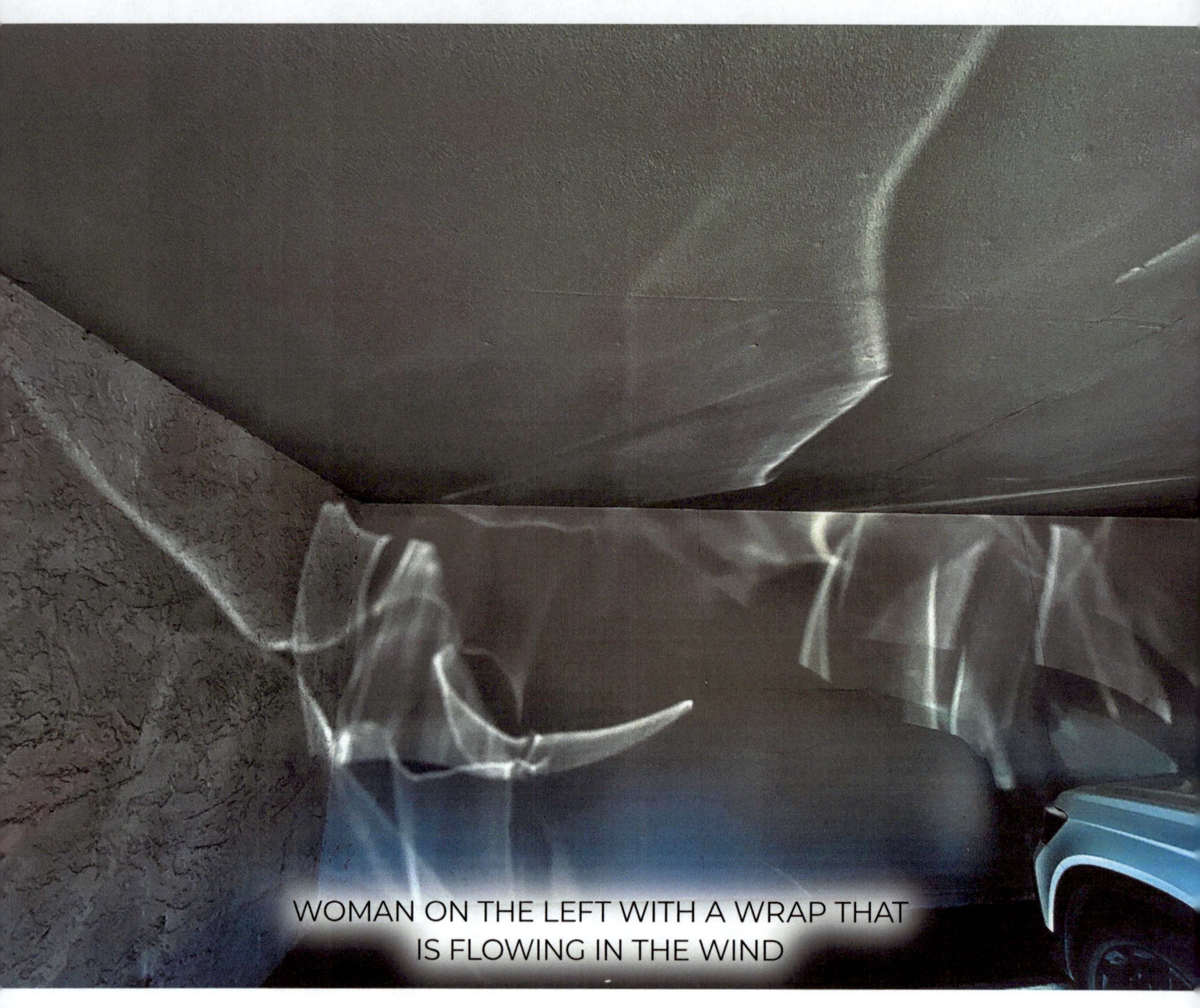
WOMAN ON THE LEFT WITH A WRAP THAT
IS FLOWING IN THE WIND

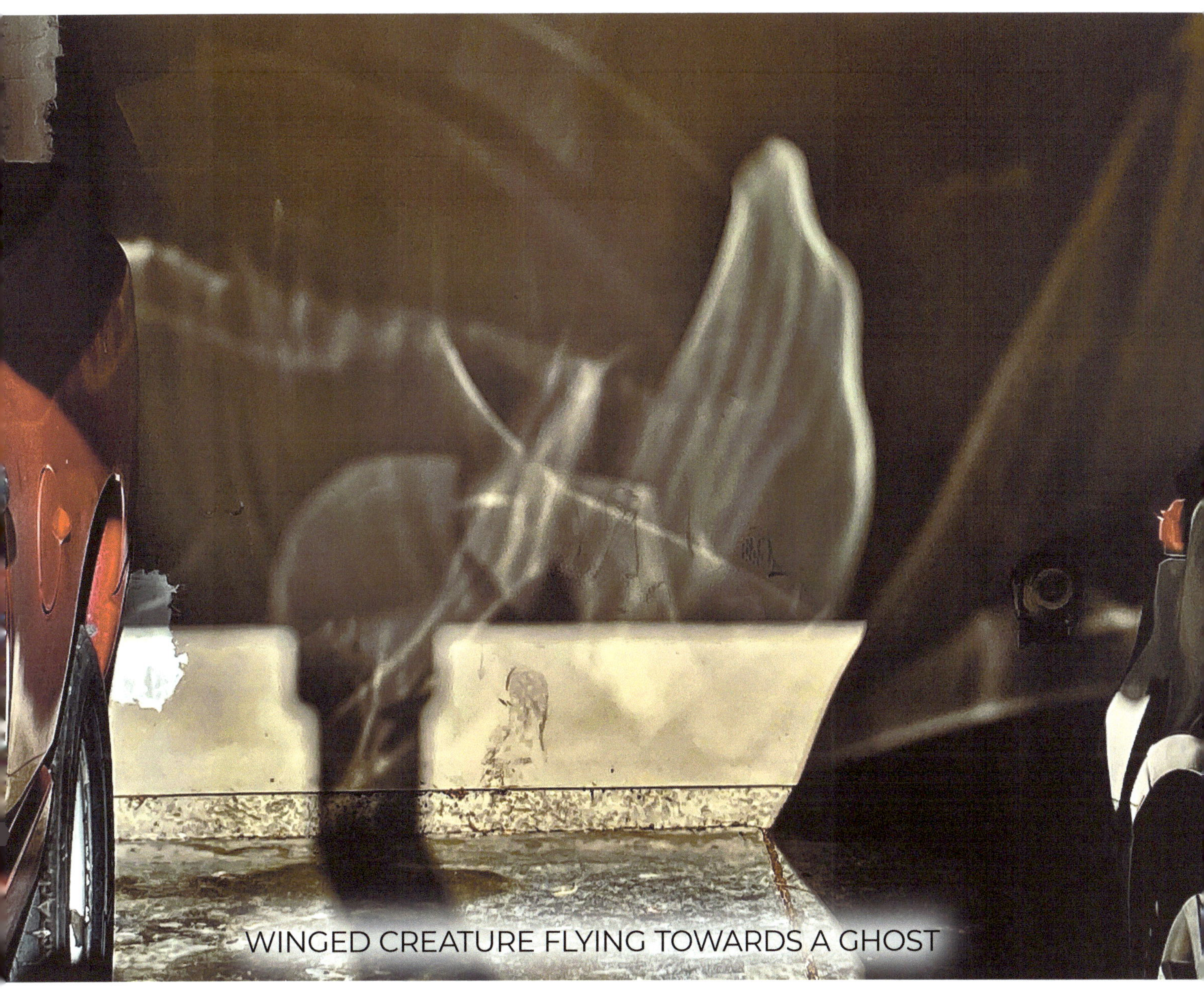

WINGED CREATURE FLYING TOWARDS A GHOST

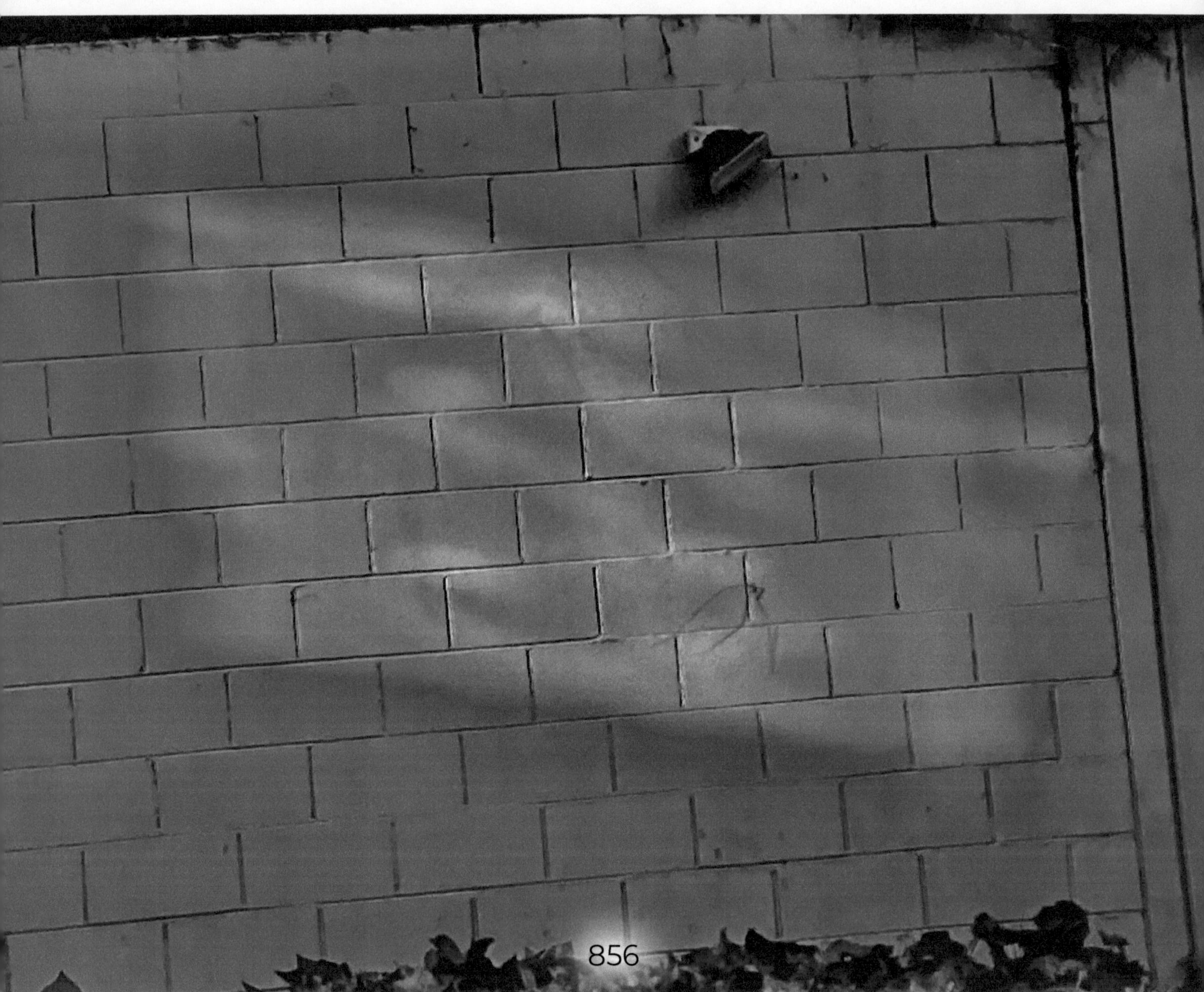

856

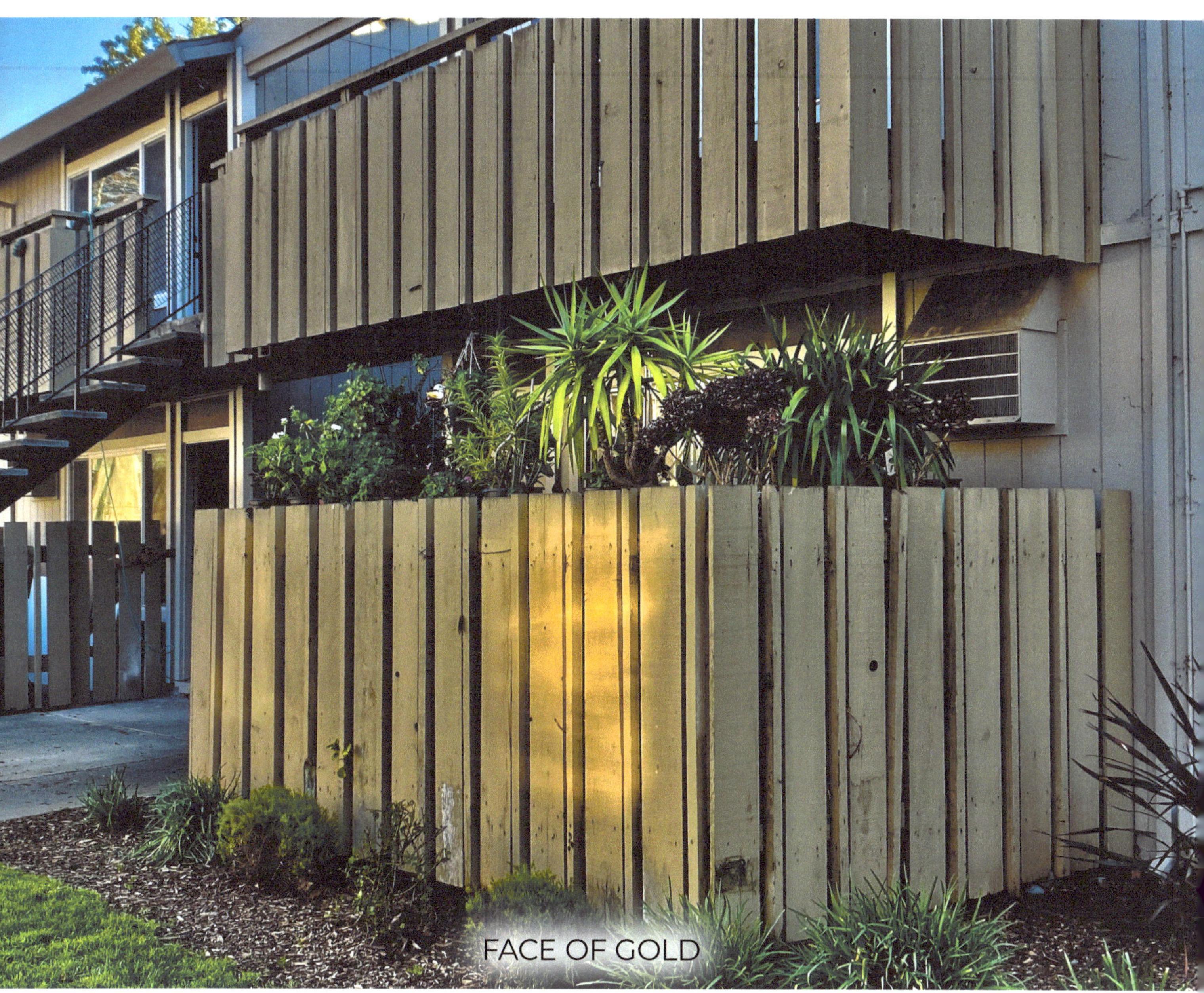
FACE OF GOLD

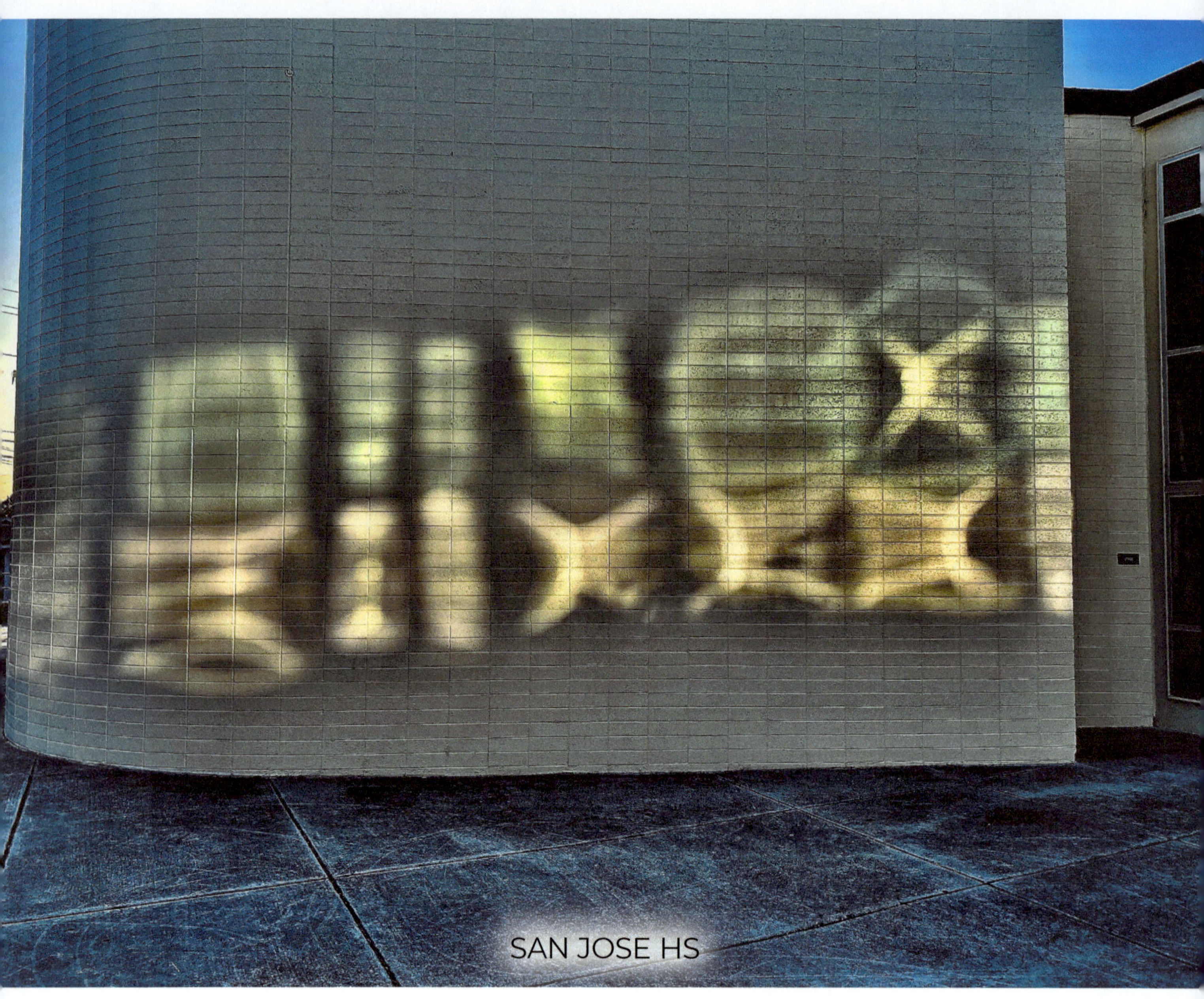

SAN JOSE HS

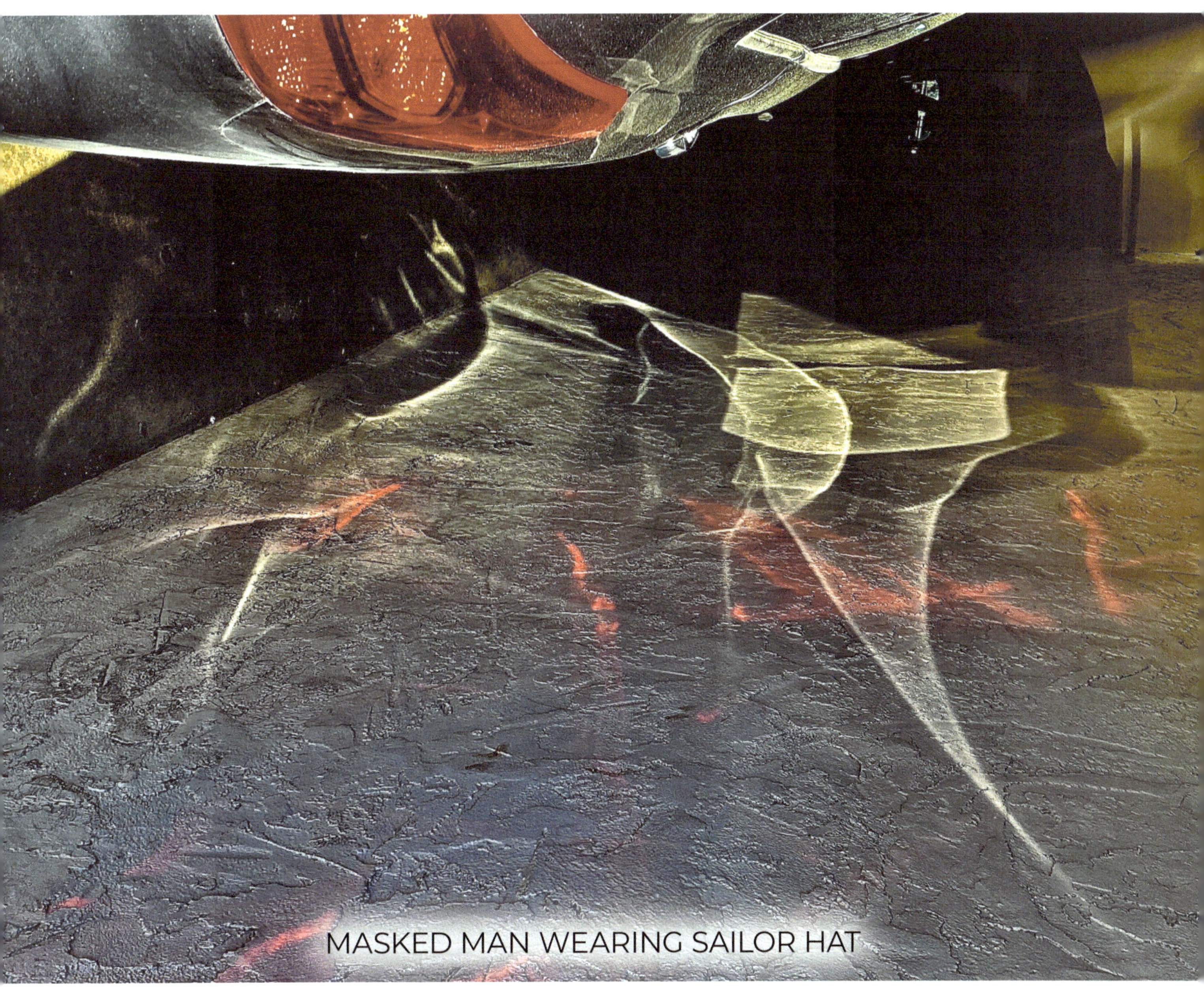

MASKED MAN WEARING SAILOR HAT

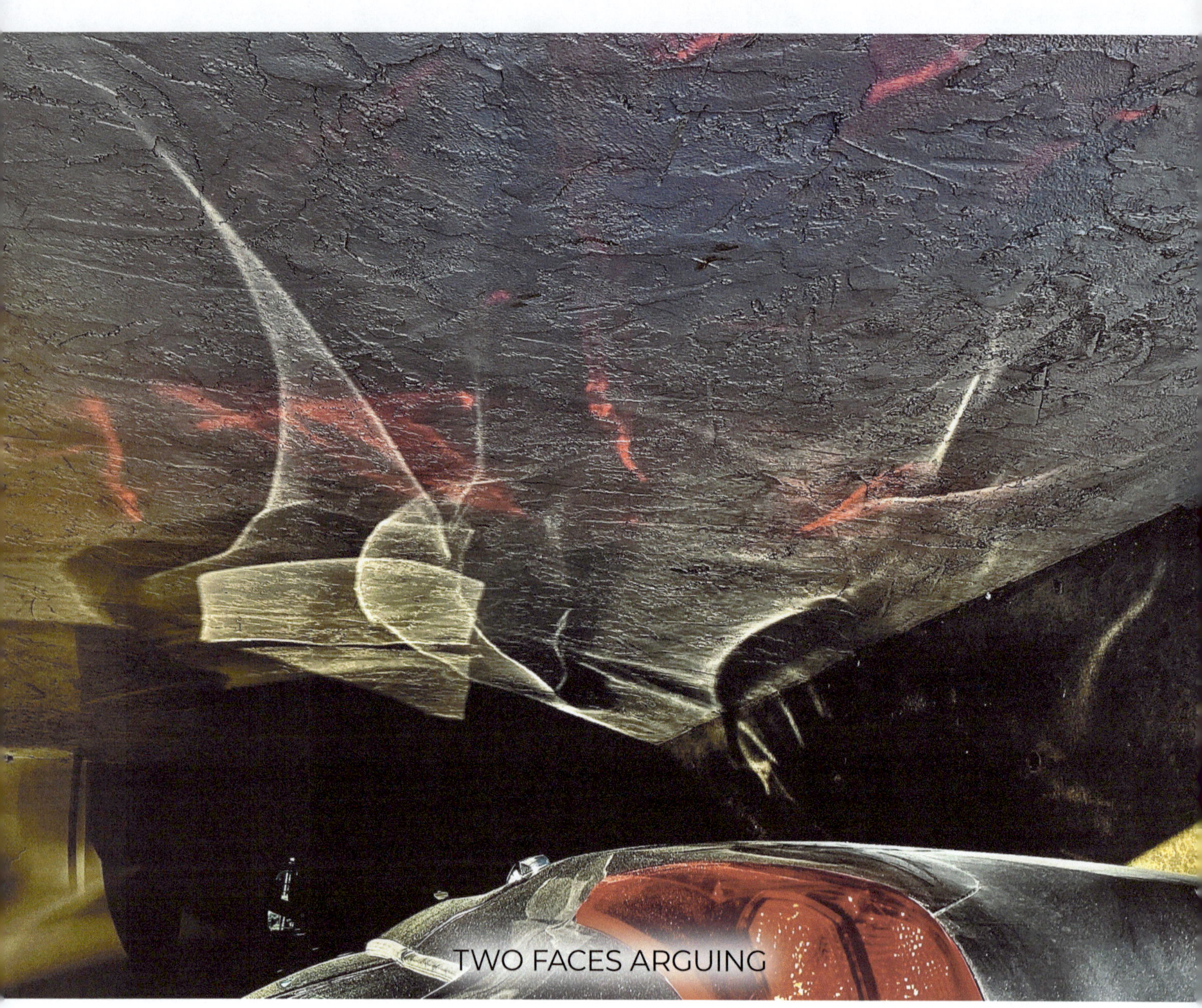
TWO FACES ARGUING

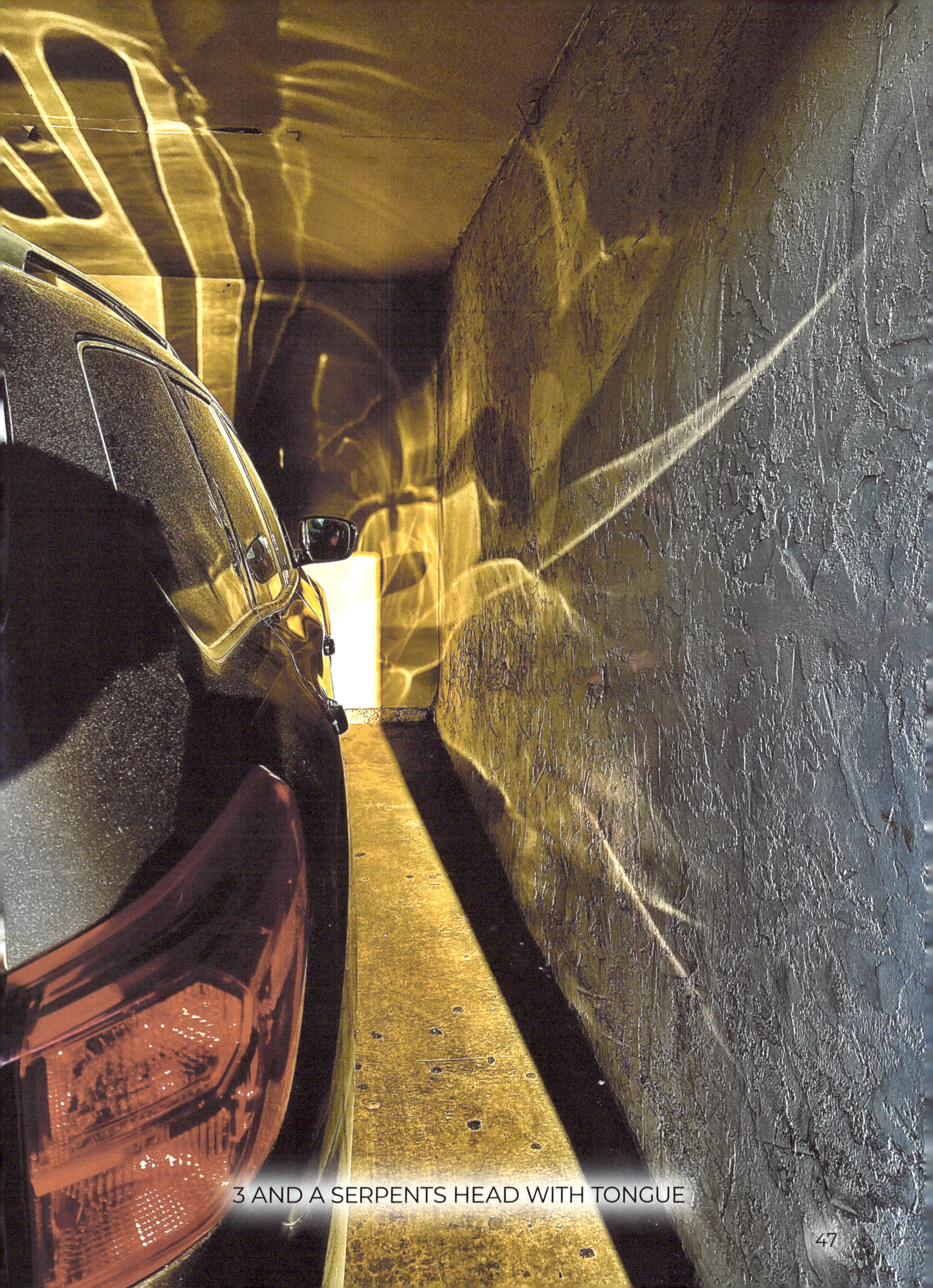
3 AND A SERPENTS HEAD WITH TONGUE

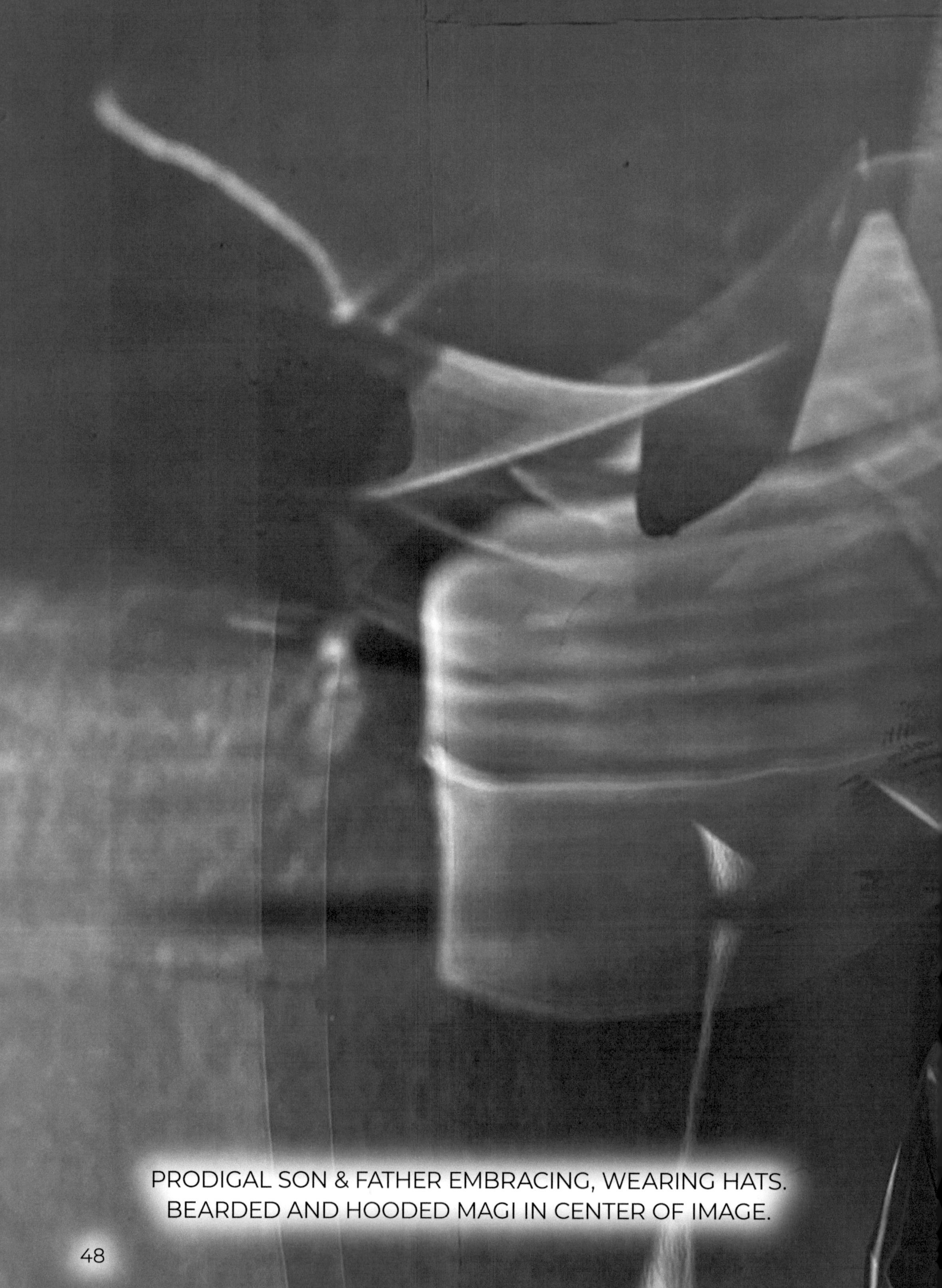

PRODIGAL SON & FATHER EMBRACING, WEARING HATS.
BEARDED AND HOODED MAGI IN CENTER OF IMAGE.

About the Author

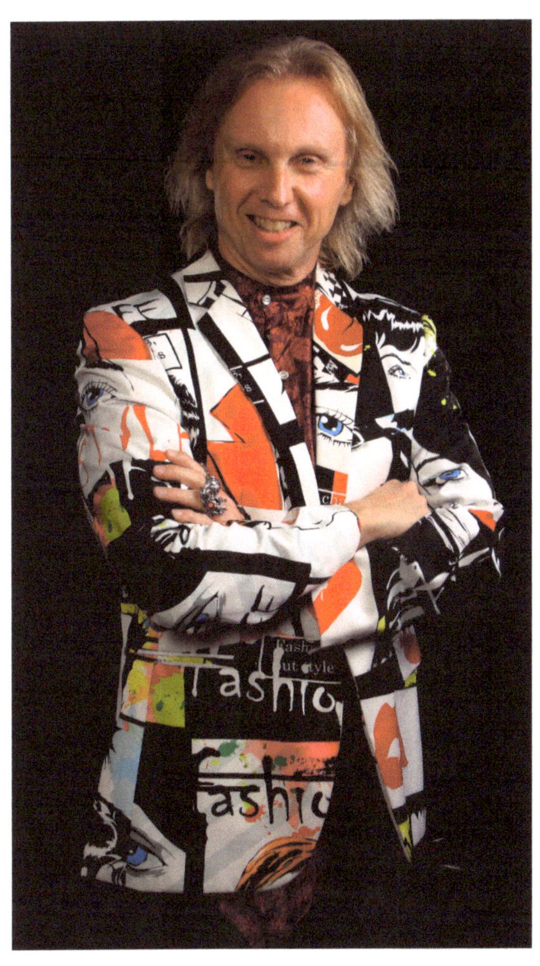

Justyn was born sometime in the last century. He believes that age is just a number and old age only happens if you allow it too. think young, speak young, speak life and not death over yourself and others. The mouth has the power of life and death, so we should use it to create and not to destroy.

He was dropped straight out of heaven and into his mothers womb. Some might even say he landed on his head upon re-entry. If that were not enough at a young age of approximately 6 while riding his bike he flew over the handlebars and landed on his head. Having been knocked unconscious he was carried home by a neighbor friend's parent, Mrs Chambers. the next two days were spent in the hospital with a concussion. A year or two later he would be accidentally hit in the head by a neighbor throwing bricks down the alley. (This may explain why he sees visions, after a few head traumas! JK)

Back in those days he was named John Pratt, by his nine year older brother. Chuck Pratt prayed him into being or existence because he was heavily outnumbered with four sisters. He has two older sisters by the names of Barb and Becky and two younger sisters by the names of Therese and Julie. Justyn is the youngest of the six siblings all born to Rosemary and Charles Pratt. Justyn was told by God to legally change his name, in the spring of 2021. It took him three months to muster the courage to change his name since he knew it was his brother who named him. He knew in his heart that family members would be disappointed or even aggravated by his decision.

But who was he to please, God or man? He chose to be obedient to God and on the day that he went to the court house, upon leaving he photographed a cloud that appeared to be a unicorn in the sky holding a bright and shining diamond upon his outstretched hoof.

Many years prior he was taught by Pastor manuel Ochoa that delayed obedience is disobedience. Justyn is very thankful for the patience of God. God's grace is sufficient for us every day. God grades on the curve of Grace! You see, Justyn had slipped into a deep dark depression after his first born daughter, Linnea Rose died at the age of 26 days. His heart was broken into a million pieces that day. Fifteen years after the death of his first born daughter he would look into the mirror and not recognize himself. He had turned his back on God, his wife Julie Pratt and his three boys Jonathan, David and Noah. their lives had been emotionally turned upside down because their father had chosen selfishness and self centeredness for a time and a season. this situation will be better detailed in the upcoming book "Follow the Signs to your Destiny and Purpose."

The bible says draw close to God and He will draw close to you. That is exactly what Justyn did back in December of 2020. He chose to return to Jesus and ultimately meet God the Father through the love of the Son. The Holy Spirit then began guiding him once more on the journey home, back to his Fathers house. God showed up in his life just in time for him to open his eyes and turn from his wicked ways. Thus becoming a better man, husband, father, brother and friend. The journey home has been one filled with love and laughter as well as sorrow and tears. His heart was being repaired one fragment at a time. Feeling discouraged or sometimes lost on the journey. Justyn would see images first in the air via the clouds, then in the aether. As an avid photographer he began looking up, looking down and looking all around himself. He would then see images in the earth, fire and water. He now has over fifty five thousand images in his collection of The Elements. He has what he refers to as proof of the spirit world working constantly all around us every moment of every day in The Elements. Now two and a half years into the process of drawing close to God, he is healing. Recognizing the darkness within, but choosing the light. Processing the grief, moving through the pain and use of the choices made. He embraced the dark shadows and sat with them for a moment in time. He has learned self love and forgiveness. He has through it all chosen to remain positive, because after all is said and done Positivity is a Super Power! He has leveled up his game and embraced self awareness.

He has chosen obedience to the first and greatest commandment: To love God with your whole heart, mind and soul. The second commandment is to love your neighbor as yourself. God is the artist of Justyn's heart and soul. Justyn is the photographer and artist that God chose to reveal signs and wonders too.

Justyn hopes and prays that you will find peace and love for God, yourself and others on your journey of life.